SHAKESPEARE'S COMEDIES
ALL THAT MATTERS

In memory of my aunts, Sheila, Tess and Moya O'Reilly. Their kindness and generosity not forgotten, with love and thanks.

SHAKESPEARE'S COMEDIES

Michael Scott

ALL THAT MATTERS

Contents

Preface

It is impossible to account for *all* that 'matters' in Shakespeare's comedies in such a limited space. Shakespearean comedy, however, does matter and as such is one of the areas rightly included in the All That Matters series. This book aims to demonstrate why it matters but also how it may matter differently to different people and to different audiences. It does so not by asking what the plays mean but, rather, how they work as comedies, taking six plays as examples. The first four are considered in the order in which they were written; the last two are not in chronological order, as they pose different kinds of issues in a modern context. Through an understanding of the mechanics of the play, the art of the playwright, narratives are communicated through which different meanings emerge depending on the predilections of the audience or reader or the artistic vision within the corporate and collective experience of a theatrical performance. It is this malleability that ensures the plays' sustainability over the centuries, making them still box-office successes. The examination of the six plays selected is framed by an introduction to Shakespearean comedy in general and a conclusion that looks at aspects of language and the use of song in the plays.

Quotations from the works are taken from *The RSC Shakespeare: The Complete Works*, edited by Jonathan Bate and Eric Rasmussen (Basingstoke: Macmillan, paperback edition, 2008).

Introduction: Shakespeare and comedy

The applause! delight!
the wonder of our stage!

My Shakespeare, rise

Ben Jonson

Shakespeare was a businessman. He was a poet and a dramatist, of course, the latter being where his real business lay. He worked for and with James Burbage, a carpenter entrepreneur who in 1576 had been bold enough to establish the first professional commercial theatre in London, called simply The Theatre. Shakespeare wrote plays and acted in plays, became shareholder and part of a business consortium of fellow actors that expanded the business when The Theatre closed and a new theatre, The Globe, was opened on another site in 1599. He bought a large house in his home town of Stratford-upon-Avon and acquired land and also the family coat of arms. Later he took an interest in a small indoor theatre, The Blackfriars. He died relatively young at the age of 52. Some would hold that he was an early capitalist who invested in land, some of which he enclosed, and who loaned money. This, however, may be taking the description a little too far. He was an entrepreneur and small businessman who actively worked in his business as an actor and writer. For Shakespeare there appears to have been no separation between the ownership of the means of production and the participation in the means of production. He certainly was a Christian in a country that had experienced religious upheaval since the time of Henry VIII. In his business career in theatre he took some risks but he was highly successful.

Comedy is a funny business at which Shakespeare excelled. Comedy is a gamble. It can be a disaster when it does not work, when it falls flat, failing to elicit the targeted response. Many have seen that happen to comedians throughout the ages and experienced their embarrassment. But when successful it brings its particular rewards. The death of the UK comedian Mel Smith in 2013 was headline news. The same occurred when the much-loved Richard Briers died. Both were popular on television but both had also appeared in Shakespearean drama in major productions. They were principally comic actors, though Briers also appeared in tragedy.

Comedy is a serious business, funny not only in itself but in the peculiarity of its unpredictability. As a businessman as well as a writer, Shakespeare excelled in it, writing plays for his popular audiences with titles such as 'As You Like It', 'What You Will', 'Much Ado About Nothing' and 'All's Well That Ends Well'. As we will see, the titles themselves may have been geared to the market, helping to attract audiences to the theatre.

Shakespeare excelled in developing the genre commercially but he was also interested in comedy as an art form, and he drew on antecedents from Classical Rome. At the beginning of his career, he was especially influenced by the work of the Roman dramatist Plautus. Shakespeare may not have read Greek but the underlying structure of his drama has an affinity with some of the principles advanced by Aristotle in *The Poetics*, in particular the way that both Shakespeare's tragedies and comedies progress towards a recognition scene, technically termed *anagnorisis*. That is the moment or scene in which the deceptions of the play are revealed, allowing the characters an understanding of what has previously occurred, and an opportunity to recognize mistakes, deceptions, follies.

In differing ways comedy exploits the human condition, whether physical, intellectual or spiritual, whether in the context of social interactions or organizations. It delves into relationships, exploiting what may appear as normality to those 'involved' in the action but as absurdities to those who are observing it. For instance, in Shakespeare's *As You Like It*, Touchstone comments on how ridiculous lovers can appear when he remarks:

> *I remember when I was in love, I broke my sword upon a stone and bid him take that for coming a-night to Jane Smile. And I remember the kissing of her batler* [a wooden tool used to pound or 'bat' laundry] *and the cow's dugs* [teats] *that her pretty chopt* [chapped] *hands had milked; and I remember the wooing of a peascod* [peas pod; a pun on the word 'codpiece', the area of the male leg garment covering the scrotum] *instead of her, from whom I took two cods* [sexual pun on testicles] *and, giving her them again, said with weeping tears, 'Wear these for my sake.'* [i.e. let's have sex]. *We that are true lovers run into strange capers; but as all is mortal in nature, so is all nature in love mortal in folly"* (2.4.38–44).

Touchstone uses sexual innuendo to aid the comedy but also to reveal how ridiculous love, or at least sexual desire, can be. He is the 'touchstone' of the play.

Comedy can also totter on the edge of melancholy and sadness in exposing human weakness or vulnerability, even in a single line as in the case of Sir Andrew Aguecheek in *Twelfth Night*, who, in one character-revealing sentence, expresses not so much his envy but his feeling of inadequacy and loneliness. He comments on Maria's love for Sir Toby with the sad but humorous line "I was adored once too" (2.3.136). It is the timing, the context and brevity of the line that creates the humour. There is a touch of brilliance about it. Today we might call this line 'Pinteresque', but Shakespeare was inaugurating the model 400 years before Pinter was born.

Ironically, academia has traditionally treated comedy as an inferior genre. Literary criticism over the years has tended to foreground tragedy as the philosophical and therefore superior dramatic genre, whether considering the Greeks or the Elizabethans. In the late 20th and early 21st centuries, some critics and scholars, including John Russell Brown, Stanley Wells and myself, have made a concerted effort to consider dramatic texts not as 'Literature' but as blueprints for performance. Such critics do not deny the literary qualities of the works, but note that however important the Shakespearean texts are as literary artefacts, they are actually incomplete. They can only come to life and to a fullness of expression when they are acted out on stage or in a studio, through the medium of film and television, or in the creative imagination of the reader.

This approach, however, can lead to other literary critical problems. Some predominant trends in recent literary evaluation, in particular New Historicism, have depended upon historical research to situate the texts within the social and political conditions of their creation. Whilst Shakespeare was hailed by Ben Jonson as the "Soul of the age!", his works were also deemed by Jonson to be "for all time!"[1]. New Historicist critics have tried to introduce a corrective to this by focusing the meaning and significance of his plays on the historical period of their composition, paying attention not just to literary but also to non-literary texts of the period. In doing so they have augmented a literary critical path with instructive historical research. Most, but not all, Cultural Materialists have done this, but from a perspective of their own Marxist-influenced methodologies, and have been overtly transparent in doing so. Other traditional and liberal humanist literary critics have questioned whether such transparency avoids misreading. They have questioned whether some of the detailed historical and sociological research on certain aspects of the Elizabethan age have always proved as useful as claimed in helping to interpret the plays.

New Historicist research, however, has been illuminating and has produced new perspectives on the plays. Studies of Shakespeare's life and time have been plentiful over the last 20 years or so in the wake of New Historicist writings such as Greenblatt's *Shakespearean Negotiations* or Cultural Materialists' work such as Malcolm Evans' *Signifying Nothing* and Jonathan Dollimore and Alan Sinfield's collection *Political Shakespeare*. A useful collection of such perspectives are found in *Alternative Shakespeares*, whilst a defensive corrective from a traditional position is argued in Brian Vickers' *Appropriating Shakespeare: Contemporary Critical Quarrels*. In the new millennium, historical studies have taken a more focused position relating to the dramatist. This is exemplified by James Shapiro's work, including *1599: A Year in the Life of William Shakespeare*, or more traditionally by Jonathan Bate's *Soul of the Age: The Life, Mind and World of William Shakespeare* or, from a feminist point of view, by Germaine Greer's *Shakespeare's Wife*.

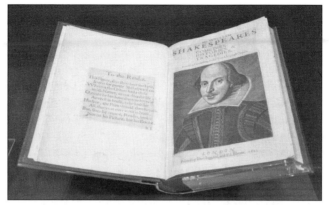

▲ The First Folio, the first collection of Shakespeare's works, brought together by his fellow actors John Heminges and Henry Condell in 1623.

But all of this, however inspiring and scholarly, can drift away from the concept of the text as a blueprint for performance. Shakespeare's scripts are not dead texts or mere historical artefacts for academia. They continue to live through being recreated and interpreted in every performance. They thereby have a life of their own, determined not just by the history of their composition, nor even their production history, but by contemporary interpretation according to modern ideologies, ideas, concepts, feelings, traditions, behaviour, understandings. The play texts are necessarily of their age but simultaneously in performance they are also of our age. Even at London's contemporary Globe Theatre, which replicates an Elizabethan public stage, an historical interpretative production cannot escape from the fact that it is being performed by 21st-century actors to 21st-century audiences made up of people who have different understandings of life and of love and its conventions than did the Elizabethans.

In *Talking Shakespeare*, I refer to Michel Foucault's statement in *The Archaeology of Knowledge*:

> *The affirmation that the earth is round or that species evolve does not constitute the same statement before and after Copernicus, before or after Darwin; it is not, for such simple formulations, that the meaning of the words has changed; what changed was the relation of these affirmations to other propositions, their conditions of use and re-investment, the field of experience, of possible verifications, of problems to be resolved, to which they can be referred[2].*

In doing so, however, I note that such an understanding of a performance script has to go further than the text itself. I write:

> *The complexity of meanings … goes beyond the text, since language in drama is not circumscribed by words. Shakespeare's language goes beyond his poetry and prose to the communication of the actions of the play, the semiotics of the drama and its narrative[3].*

Such actions are not frozen in time, they are represented and created anew each time the script goes into performance. Consequently both the words and the action of the play embody and reflect changing meanings as time passes. Many initially successful plays may become dated or obsolete but certain plays have the malleability in their texts to allow for reinterpretation because they have an existence as performance scripts that finds their meanings in the context of the age, the society, the individual and the dominant ideologies and resistances that pertain at any particular time.

The concept of a living Shakespeare, a script for production, makes us, even in the study, look at how the mechanics of the plays work, their underpinning structure, relationship with plot and the exposure of theme through harmony or discord or a combination of both. Consequently in this short book on Shakespeare's comedies, I am concentrating on how the plays work through the inbuilt tensions or resolutions deriving from a structural platform that Shakepeare used time and time again to create his comic plays. This structural platform or formula, used for many Shakespearean comedies, has four broad elements:

1 An opening statement(s) of dilemmas or seemingly impossible social difficulties, often but not always associated with the threat of death.

2 A search involved with the opening statement and relating, firstly, to an individual (or a number of individuals) attempting to find identity or self-knowledge, and secondly, to one or more couples (usually young) attempting to develop their relationships with each other.

3 The requirement of the searchers to remove themselves from the society which formed the opening statement – that removal being signified in the plays from 1595 onwards by geographical relocation or physical disguise or both.

4 Through the adventures while disguised or in the area of relocation, a movement towards a comic resolution. This usually operates structurally through, firstly, an engineered recognition scene – *anagnorisis* – in which misunderstandings of identity are revealed and realized, and secondly, through multiple marriage, which usually ensues or is confirmed through the mechanism of the recognition scene.

From that generic structural platform, plots develop which explore the different ramifications of this formula. So in *Twelfth Night*, for example, the plot follows the structure:

1 Orsino self-indulgently loves Olivia but she indulgently mourns the death of her father and brother and refuses to return his love. Meanwhile, a girl (Viola) is shipwrecked, her twin brother (Sebastian) being lost at sea. She determines to serve the love-stricken duke of the land where she has been stranded.

2 The search for Viola's own identity and the search for Orsino's and Olivia's self-knowledge involves Viola disguising herself as a young man who is accepted at both Orsino's court and Olivia's house.

3 Adventures and further misunderstandings accrue as both Olivia and Orsino form an attachment for 'Cesario', the disguised Viola.

4 These adventures are concluded by the engineered recognition scene – *anagnorisis* – when the lost twin brother, Sebastian, arrives and, recognizing Cesario's likeness to him, says: "Do I stand there?".

The dialogue progresses to prove to each other and to those around them who they are. The errors of the play are thereby corrected and in conclusion there follows an affirmation of the multiple marriage. Olivia has unwittingly already married Sebastian but confirms her love, Orsino marries Viola, and the characters Sir Toby and Maria are revealed to have just married too.

Similarly, in *As You Like It* there is an initial discord between two brothers, Oliver and Orlando de Bois, leading to a threat of death, and between the usurper Duke Frederick and his deposed brother Duke Senior, who is exiled in the Forest of Arden. This leads to a search for a new life for Duke Senior and Duke Senior's daughter and niece, Rosalind and Celia, who disguise themselves, Rosalind as a man, Ganymede, *"Because that I am more than common tall"* (1.3.111) and Celia as a poor young maid, Aliena (i.e. a stranger, or not herself). Orlando and the old family servant Adam also escape to the forest. There, adventures occur in the search for true identity, which Rosalind resolves through an engineered recognition scene. Hymen, the god of marriage, fictionally – in a masque within the play – appears to present Rosalind to her father and to Orlando (5.4.84–92).

Other marriages of characters to whom we have been introduced in the action are confirmed by Hymen: *"Here's eight that must take hands/To join in Hymen's bands"* (5.4.101–2). Celia is married to Oliver, Phoebe to Silvius, and Audrey to Touchstone, complementing Rosalind's marriage to Orlando. News arrives that Duke

Frederick, on entering the forest, has become full of remorse and has gone to live a religious life, allowing Duke Senior and others – with the notable exception of the malcontent Jaques – to return to their original status and location.

So Shakespeare creates both structure and plot, but it is within the relationship of the two that we find not merely a story but a thematic narrative that embraces individuals, society and the conduct of living. In *As You Like It* this springs from two confrontations, the one between the two dukes which has occurred 'before the play has started', i.e. which is given to us as information to help establish the plot; the second is between the two brothers Oliver and Orlando, which is of such ferocity on Oliver's part that he seeks not just separation from but the death of his brother. Similarly, in *Twelfth Night*, the audience is provided with the revelation from the start of Orsino's infatuation (which is more to do with self-gratification than with love) and with the exposure of Olivia's self-indulgence in her excessive mourning. This is ridiculed early in the play by the comic audacity of the Fool, Feste:

Feste: *Good madonna, why mourn'st thou?*
Olivia: *Good fool, for my brother's death.*
Feste: *I think his soul is in hell, madonna.*
Olivia: *I know his soul is in heaven, fool.*
Feste: *The more fool, madonna, to mourn your brother's soul being in heaven. Take away the fool, gentlemen.*
            (1.5.49–54)

Feste's intervention here is emblematic of the Fool's function across a number of plays, both comic and tragic, in being a touchstone to the reality depicted in the play and the issues it raises, stripping back pretentions, hypocrisy and self-delusion. In *King Lear*, the king's fool sings a different stanza from the song with which Feste closes *Twelfth Night*. In the midst of storm and tempest, both in King Lear's mind as well as in the elements, the Fool cries:

He that has and a little tiny wit,
With hey, ho, the wind and the rain,
Must make content with his fortunes fit,
Though the rain it raineth every day. (3.2. 73–6)

Later, as Lear tears off his clothes, the Fool advises:

Prithee, nuncle, be contented: 'tis a naughty night to swim in. Now a little fire in a wild field were like an old lecher's heart, a small spark, all the rest on's body cold. (3.4.91–3)

The Fool's function in the plays is to try to dispel self-deception by exposing the realties of nature: the rain, the cold, the need for clothes. The world, the body and even a play function through their intrinsic structures. Break those aspects and chaos ensues, whether it be in comedy through, for example, the self-gratification and deception of Orsino in *Twelfth Night*, or through the self-destructive conditions of the tragedies. The Fool's final stanza in *Twelfth Night* draws the parallel with the stage:

A great while ago the world begun,
With hey, ho, (the wind and the rain)

But that's all one, our play is done,
And we'll strive to please you every day. (5.1.387–90)

The subplots of the plays fulfil a similar functional role in that they mirror elements of the main plot in order to take forward thematic points. We might think in this context of Malvolio's self-indulgence and infatuation, which becomes the butt of a cruel practical joke in *Twelfth Night*, or of the relationship between the Oberon–Titania quarrel in *A Midsummer Night's Dream* and the quarrels in the same play involving Lysander, Hermia, Demetrius and Helena in the forest, or the seeming tension at court between Theseus and Hippolita over the dilemma of the young lovers. Some scholars, moreover, might consider the quality of a play to be found in the artist accomplishing the harmonious interlocking of structure that imbues the plot with a thematic consistency.

To achieve that perfect relationship, even if desired, is rare even for Shakespeare. In *The Comedy of Errors*, Shakespeare uses a neoclassical structure but in so doing, starts to develop his own functional structure for comedy. Even at this early stage, however, in the final act of the play the dramatist has to bring on, for the first time, Egeon's long-lost wife, making her the abbess of the local convent in order to create a rather forced, though still amusing, recognition scene. In *As You Like It*, a third brother (Jaques de Bois, the second son of Rowland de Bois) is introduced suddenly in the final scene of the play to round the plot off in a rather clumsy way, although despite its awkwardness it usually gains a sympathetic laugh from the audience. They have probably forgotten that he was mentioned at the start of the play as he doesn't appear on stage until half way through the final scene. The powerful quality of the complex relationships that the play explores counterbalance the artificiality of such a forced device. But the detail has been established at an earlier stage as part of the process of the play itself. By the ending, therefore, we can laugh at this artificiality since the play's more complex structural motifs have already made more than their mark.

In *The Comedy of Errors*, *Love's Labour's Lost*, *The Two Gentlemen of Verona* and *A Midsummer Night's Dream*, the thematic concerns in terms of characterization or subplot may not be developed to the extent that we find them in *The Merchant of Venice*, *Twelfth Night* or *As You Like It*. In *A Midsummer Night's Dream*, however, they are used to develop a satire on theatrical activity itself and in doing so to expose, through the lower orders of society, some of the pretensions of the aristocrats. The same occurs in *Love's Labour's Lost*, where the aristocrats show little regard, except in a rather patronizing way, for the attempts of ordinary people trying to do their best in pleasing their 'betters'. The clown, here named Costard, once again provides a corrective perspective by expressing a balance between what can be laughed at and a sympathy with the qualities of the person being ridiculed. He defends Sir Nathaniel, the curate, who is being laughed at by the courtiers in his tongue-tied attempt to play the part of Alexander the Great. Costard comments:

> A conqueror and afraid to speak? Run away for shame,
> Alisander. There, an't shall please you, a foolish mild

man, an honest man, look you, and soon dashed. He is a marvellous good neighbour, in sooth, and a very good bowler. But for Alisander, alas, you see how 'tis – a little o'erparted. (5.2.597–601)

Love's Labour's Lost does not follow the functional structure used in the later romantic comedies but nevertheless can be seen to incorporate aspects of it through its plot. The King of Navarre vows a contemplative life of study for three years and elicits a similar sacrifice from his lords Berowne, Longaville and Dumain, although Berowne complains:

> *O, these are barren tasks, too hard to keep:*
> *Not to see ladies, study, fast, not sleep.* (1.1.47–8)

"Too hard" it soon proves to be, as a female embassy led by the Princess of France arrives to meet with King Ferdinand and love interferes with this diplomatic mission. The men resort to performing masques themselves, and encourage the people of the town to assist them in their courting of the ladies and to support their collective comic hypocrisy. But love in reality proves not to be so frivolous. The news of the death of the King of France at the end of the play introduces a stark reality into their pretentious, perjured fooling. King Ferdinand and his courtiers have to share the harsh lesson of the reality that has intruded upon their playing. The King is sentenced for 12 months to a "naked hermitage, / Remote from all the pleasures of the world" (5.2.793–4) before the Princess will marry him, whilst Berowne is sentenced by Rosaline's judgement to make sick people happy with his jesting for, "a twelvemonth in an hospital"

(5.2.870). The other two courtiers also have to wait a year before they can expect to marry their loves. Ridiculous vows and the frivolous circumstances of the courtiers are placed against the reality and fragility of life. The play is usually dated to 1595–6. Shakespeare's young son, Hamnet, died in August 1596. That is the reality of life and death outside the theatre.

It may be that in the early plays, and even up to *As You Like It* and beyond, Shakespeare found complexity in resolving all his plots without structural artifice. As I discuss in *Renaissance Drama and a Modern Audience*, in *Measure for Measure* (1604) it appears that there is a deliberate jarring between structure and plot in order to gain dramatic effect. Incongruity of structure and plot creates compelling work as comic and tragic genres deliberately rub uneasily against each other. In *The Merchant of Venice* an interweaving of plots and structure results in a complex, possibly confrontational depiction of both Jewish and Christian conduct.

It is notable that there is a fine balance between the comic and the tragic effect in a play such as *Othello* (1604), a play that some regard as a comedy that has, somehow, gone wrong. Distinguished critics such as G. Wilson Knight, in *The Wheel of Fire*, and Peter Davison, in *Hamlet: Text and Performance*, have written interestingly about the comic elements of *King Lear* (1605/6) and *Hamlet* (1600). *Cymbeline* (1610) is termed a tragedy but exploits many comic devices, almost as if Shakespeare is deliberately deconstructing his comic formula in an attempt to create something new.

In *Much Ado About Nothing* (1598), we experience a play that utilizes a different structure. Here the apparently motiveless intrigues of Duke Pedro's illegitimate brother, Don John, leads to the supposed death of Hero, falsely accused of wantoness by her husband to be, Claudio. Her cousin, Beatrice, demands that if Benedick loves her, he will kill his friend Claudio to satisfy the need for revenge and justice. This potentially tragic plot is, however, resolved by a comic ending in which the 'mistake' or 'supposes' or deliberate distortions found in comic plots are revealed within a sinister atmosphere. The play looks forward to *All's Well that Ends Well* (1603/6) and *The Winter's Tale* (1611) in this respect but there are structural and narrative echoes here also with the tragedy *Othello* (1604). Indeed, Shakespeare reuses devices and motifs that occur first in *Much Ado*, but whose tragic and tragicomic potential are later explored in *Othello* and *The Winter's Tale* respectively.

Romeo and Juliet (1595/6) is particularly interesting in the context of an early comedy/tragedy mix. Much of its early action is romantically comic or at least appears so. Romeo initially proclaims his love for Rosaline but falls in love with Juliet during a prank which exploits the feud between the two houses of Montague and Capulet. The social context of that enmity in the city, however, is manifested in the continual threat of violence that pervades the play from the start. It is relieved at first by the comic taunting of Mercutio, who provokes and teases. His famous 'Queen Mab' speech (1.4.55–97) has a dream-like quality found in a more extended form in many of the comedies discussed in later chapters. Some may regard this quality as part of the Renaissance humanist's search for, or affirmation of, the concrete uniqueness of a character's being and feelings. This privileging of the individual within his or her experience of the human world, or the universe, can encompass even the fairyland of Queen Mab in *Romeo and Juliet* or, for that matter, Oberon and Titania in *A Midsummer Night's Dream*. In comedy, this search for a humanist identity may lead to the recognition of all the mistakes and illusions and a reconciliation that is fundamentally social in its emphasis upon how the energies of society can be replenished from one generation to the next. In tragedy, it leads to death. But beyond that, is there, we might ask, a breakdown of rationality at work within the individual, or that extends beyond the conscious life of the individual, that Shakespeare articulates through the metaphor of a dream which parallels the nature of a play? In one of Shakespeare's final plays, *The Tempest* (1611), Prospero remarks:

We are such stuff
As dreams are made on; and our little life
Is rounded with a sleep. (4.1.169–71)

Prospero does so through utilizing the metaphor of a play, having previously shown a masque to the young lovers Ferdinand and Miranda. Life is transitory, and once completed, all is over like a performance of a play. Once any performance is concluded, it is gone, finished, as if evaporated into the air:

> *Our revels now are ended. These our actors,*
> *As I foretold you, were all spirits and*
> *Are melted into air, into thin air,*
> *And, like the baseless fabric of this vision,*
> *The cloud-capped towers, the gorgeous palaces,*
> *The solemn temples, the great globe itself,*
> *Yea, all which it inherit, shall dissolve,*
> *And, like this insubstantial pageant faded,*
> *Leave not a rack behind.* (4.1.161–9)

Such is the theatre and its artefacts, like a dream, but also like life itself. *The Tempest*, now usually termed a 'last play' or even, most recently by the Royal Shakespeare Company (RSC), a 'shipwreck' play, was originally categorized as a comedy and placed as the first of the plays printed in the First Folio (1623). Then, as now, comedy was more than just a funny business.

The Comedy of Errors (1592–4)

*He that commends me to mine
own content*

*Commends me to the thing
I cannot get.*

(1.2.33–4)

If the early play *The Two Gentlemen of Verona* (1590–2) is an experimental one by a young dramatist striving to find a workable structure and plot, *The Comedy of Errors* (1594) demonstrates the first phase of success. Stanley Wells has noted that although it has usually been considered in the context of an early play, *The Comedy of Errors* has an artistry in its construction that possibly belies this belief. He writes:

> *The plotting of* The Comedy of Errors *is an intellectual feat of some magnitude, akin to the composition of a fugue. But it is also characteristic of Shakespeare to broaden the play's emotional range by adding the wholly serious framework, derived from another classical story which he was to use again close to the end of his career in Pericles ...*[4]

Wells is referring here to the two classical sources for the work, *The Brothers Menaechmi* and *The Amphitruo* by the Roman playwright Plautus, and additionally the old romance *Appollonius of Tyre* which was the principal source of *Pericles* (1608), a play written by Shakespeare in partnership with George Wilkins. But there are further influences on the play; Shakespeare moves the plot of his source story from Epidamnus to Ephesus, known to his audience from the Acts of the Apostles as well as from St Paul's letter to the Ephesians.

Knowing one's audience and market is the business of the theatrical practitioner. Shakespeare's theatre, no less than London's current West End or New York's Broadway, was a commercial enterprise, although at this moment in its history the public theatre was more than simply a commodity. It required judgement and skill in the decision of what to present and when to do it, as well as an awareness of what the authorities were prepared to tolerate.

Eight or nine years before *The Comedy of Errors* was written, England was at war with Spain and the Armada had set sail to invade English shores and remove its monarch. Although storms and foul weather and the ships of Hawkins and Drake had been able to defeat the Armada, more people died in the following period of plague, starvation and poverty-related disease than in the Armada itself. This is a part of history that traditionally has not been celebrated, for obvious reasons. It was during this period, however, that Shakespeare arrived in London from Stratford and began to write his plays. His *Henry VI* plays examined the weakness of monarchy and the cruelty of civil unrest as an ever-pressing danger in Elizabeth's reign. These were to set the young dramatist up for a series of history plays throughout the 1590s, during a period of great uncertainty about the succession to the throne should the ageing and childless queen die. In the Elizabethan age, death could be around the corner, the great leveller striking rich or poor through plague, disease or violence with little warning; during the composition of this play, the plague in 1592 resulted in the closure of the theatres for two years. Indeed, whenever plague deaths reached 40 a week in London, the theatres were closed, and commentators have speculated that on some of these occasions Shakespeare and his company may have toured the provinces.

Shakespeare's history plays helped to make the dramatist's name and reputation. He apparently became a young dramatist of renown and, after Christopher Marlowe's violent death in May 1593, Shakespeare was to develop into one of the most prominent dramatists of his time. There were other candidates, of course, in the competitive world of the theatre business. Indeed, in the early stages of his life as a dramatist he was criticized by a fellow dramatist, Robert Greene, as an "upstart crow, beautified with our feathers", in other words, living off other dramatists' ideas and texts. It would have been surprising if he had not. Ask a successful 21st-century businessman if it's better to come up with the original business idea or to be the 'fast second' into the market and most will reply the latter.

With *The Comedy of Errors* Shakespeare wove together popular Roman plays but added a further twist by creating a second set of identical twins. Some might call this a stroke of commercial genius. It certainly was the ingenuity of a dramatist establishing himself on the theatrical scene and going for what today we term a box-office hit by creating an innovative farce to make people laugh.

Farce depends on timing and skill and the audience's prior knowledge of principal elements of the story which the characters either fail to recognize or try hard to conceal. The audience is thereby invited to enjoy the confusions that arise, secure in the knowledge that in the end all the misunderstandings and misconceptions will be revealed. So from the start the audience is made to feel secure in what they are going to witness. In this, the audience isn't passive since that security allows them to laugh at the action, which in turn encourages the actors to exaggerate their predicaments as the confusions multiply. Farce depends on the audience's laughter as well as on the dexterity of the dramatist and the comic timing of the actors. In adapting the Plautine model to create the two sets of twins named Antipholus and Dromio, Shakespeare increased his chance of success. The story of the two sets is told at the beginning of the play by the father of the Antipholus twins, Egeon, an aged Syracusian merchant who has arrived at the town of Ephesus to find it at war with Syracuse. He has been arrested and summarily sentenced to death by the Duke of Ephesus, Solinus. The absurdity of his story becomes apparent when Solinus asks Egeon to tell the motivation and the history of his travels. The old man begins:

A heavier task could not have been imposed
Than I to speak my griefs unspeakable.
Yet, that the world may witness that my end
Was wrought by nature, not by vile offence,
I'll utter what my sorrow gives me leave. (1.1.31–5)

He then narrates how his wife, whilst travelling with him years ago, gave birth to *"two goodly sons, / ... the one so like the other, / As could not be distinguished but by names"* (1.1.49, 50–2). He continues that at the very same hour *"and in the self-same inn, / A poor mean woman was deliveréd / Of such a burden, male twins, both alike"* (1.1.53–5).

The audience thus has been given the principal ingredient of the farce to come. Egeon's fantastical tale goes on to explain how he and his wife bought the second set of twins from the poor woman to be servants to their own twin sons. They eventually decided to return home but "*a league from Epidamium*" a storm hit them and the ship was abandoned by the crew. Egeon's wife had fastened one of her own twins to the end of a mast along with one of the servant twins. At the other end they did the same, with the wife going to the one end, and he, the husband, to the other. As the ship sank the mast floated until the storm was over. Then in the calm they saw two ships coming towards them from different places, Corinth and Epidaurus. They would have been saved together but their mast hit a rock and broke in two, Egeon's wife's end of the mast travelled faster in the sea, and she was rescued by one of the ships and he by the other. The two rescue ships then went their separate ways without meeting, and husband and wife and the two sets of twins were thereby divorced from each other, and from themselves. The youngest son remained with Egeon but, adding to the comic potential, retained the name of the eldest, Antipholus, while the servant twins were both named Dromio.

The audience now knows that there are two sets of twins, originally only distinguished by their names but who actually have the same names. At the age of 18, the younger of the twin sons decides to go in search of the other and his father, Egeon, follows him. This is a recipe for pure comic farce given to the audience at the beginning of the play, and Shakespeare, probably early in his dramatic career, exploits this for all its worth.

It is the material for commercial theatrical success which the traditional literary establishment through the centuries has found difficult to justify. If comedy was traditionally regarded as being inferior to tragedy, then farce is placed even further down the scale. It has to be excused by literary critics and its serious nature has to be discovered. So critics of the 20th and 21st centuries have found excuses for it. L. G. Salingar pointed to the fact that there was too much serious emotion in the play for it to be considered simply a farce, whilst in his Introduction to the Arden edition of the play R. A. Foakes commented: "The fact is that the serious elements are in some danger of going unobserved, while no one is likely to miss the fun, especially in the distorted and jazzed-up versions of the play which are commonly staged."[5]

Stephen Greenblatt has continued in a similar vein, writing, for example: "Since *The Comedy of Errors* is a farce and since it is based on a Roman model that has absolutely no emotional investment in the figure of the wife ... it is all the more striking that Shakespeare registered so acutely her anguish." Greenblatt is referring to Act 2 Scene 2 lines 110–20, where Adriana, who is married to Antipholus of Ephesus, accuses him of treating her with disdain. Adriana complains about being left at home while her husband travels, and she is reminded of her duties by her unmarried sister, into whose mouth, ironically, a defence of marriage is placed. Greenblatt enlarges his argument of the seriousness of the comedy here to note that at the end of the farce "the play does not include, as it would be reasonable to expect, a scene of marital reconciliation." He concludes that this is a defect in Shakespeare himself who did not in most of his plays seem to understand what it meant really "to share a life"[6]. Greenblatt, of course, is judging the play from the standpoint of a modern relationship, whereas despite the farcical predicament in which Adriana is placed, she is part of a comic dialogue that includes a realistic discussion of the everyday tensions of contemporary Elizabethan marriage.

It is when critics start to come to such conclusions that we have to wonder whether they are falling into a trap which Chaucer described as taking in earnest what was meant for game.

Stanley Wells, on the other hand, is helpful in directing our attention to the fugue as a means of understanding the working of this play. A fugue starts with a phrase of music which becomes complicated by the same phrase being repeated and in the process accumulating layers that produce a richness of sound. In this play, once we have been told the fantastic story of Egeon, Shakespeare introduces us to the two sets of twins who are now in Ephesus: the one set being of Ephesus, the other of Syracuse. He proceeds to mix people up in a series of confusions and mistakes involving the two servants, the wife and her sister, a courtesan, a goldsmith, a creditor, two merchants, a kitchen maid, a schoolmaster and an exorcist named Dr Pinch. The result is confusion as the mistaken identities proliferate, to the delight of an audience that is always 'in the know'. Yet, within all of this confusion and mayhem, the issue of identity breaks through and it is here that Shakespeare adds a further innovative dimension to the drama in terms of characterization. In Act 1 Scene 2, the merchant of Ephesus who has warned Antipholus of Syracuse that he is in danger, because Ephesus is engaged in a trade war with Syracuse, leaves him to his "*own content*" till they might meet later. The phrase gives Antipholus a cue:

He that commends me to mine own content
Commends me to the thing I cannot get.
I to the world am like a drop of water
That in the ocean seeks another drop,
Who, falling there to find his fellow forth –
Unseen, inquisitive – confounds himself.
So I, to find a mother and a brother,
In quest of them, unhappy, lose myself. (1.2.33-40)

This brilliant extemporized repetition of a musical phrase deepens the drama to provide a fleetingly melancholic insight into one of the characters who will be the unwitting cause of the ensuing confusion. The same is true of Adriana, Antipholus of Ephesus's wife, who suspects her husband of marital infidelity and asks her sister, Luciana, "Why should their liberty than ours be more?" (2.1.10) The confusion over the twin Antipholuses is allowed by the dramatist to expose marital problems, which increases the humour because it touches on issues with which an audience can empathize. So when Adriana rebukes Antipholus of Syracuse, thinking him to be her husband, the painful truths that she reveals about her marriage are placed within a comic context, since the man she is chastising is not her husband:

Ay, ay, Antipholus, look strange and frown.
Some other mistress hath thy sweet aspects.
I am not Adriana nor thy wife. (2.2.101-3)

This ironic 'error', of course, is part of the fun of the encounter, but the poignancy of her comments derives from the fact that she thinks that she is upbraiding her husband by confronting him with a bitter truth. Evidently, her actual husband does not treat her as a wife might reasonably expect to be treated and this introduces an element of melancholy into the comic layering of the action that serves only to deepen the overall comic effect of the scene. It is startling, accomplished and innovative writing.

With the confusions or 'errors', Shakespeare introduces further elements that add significantly to the theme of loss of identity and the male/female relationships involving sister-in-law and courtesan as well as husband and wife. These other issues arise from the inability of the characters to rationalize what is occurring, because none are in possession of all of the facts at any one time. No one stands back and considers why the world has become for them so confused. Instead they continually resort to threats of violence, to magic or to the law. The Dromios are constantly chastised and beaten because of what they truthfully say to the wrong Antipholus. Antipholus of Ephesus calls for a crowbar and a rope in order to break into his home, from which he has been locked out by a wife who thinks that she has already got her husband indoors. Antipholus of Syracuse, now the recipient of his brother's wife's favours, is already convinced by his earlier experiences of Ephesus that the strange land where he has arrived is ruled by wickedness and wizardry:

They say this town is full of cozenage,
As nimble jugglers that deceive the eye,
Dark-working sorcerers that change the mind,
Soul-killing witches that deform the body,
Disguisèd cheaters, prating mountebanks,
And many suchlike liberties of sin (1.2.97–102).

By Act 4 Scene 4, the Courtesan, Adriana and Luciana all consider Antipholus of Ephesus to have gone mad, and the ridiculous schoolmaster Dr Pinch is engaged as an exorcist to try to bring him to his senses. By Act 5 Scene 1, Antipholus of Syracuse and the second Merchant confront each other in a swordfight, until Dromio calls his master to take refuge in a priory.

The discipline of the multi-layering fugue-like quality of the action compounds the irrational behaviour into comic chaos. Stage props such as ropes, money and jewellery circulate among the actors to provide the tangible material out of which jokes are fabricated; the delivery of these objects to the wrong destinations provides material for an increasingly fast-paced plot, and as the layers of confusion build up, rationality fails time and again to produce answers to the characters' dilemmas. An Abbess in Act 5 Scene 1 enters into the confusion and scolds the wife, Adriana, over the way she has reproached her husband, Antipholus of Ephesus. In addition to the husband/wife motif, Shakespeare now adds a daughter-in-law/mother-in-law motif, except that until the very end of the play neither party knows who the other is. The only structural issue with this, however, is that the true identity of the Abbess is withheld from the audience, although, as in the case of the final destination of the sum of money that circulates throughout the play (and that will be the price of Egeon's life), they may well guess, but the recognition is still to come. That recognition comes in two parts. The first is when the Abbess (Emilia) re-enters the stage with Antipholus and Dromio of Syracuse to confront Duke Solinus, who is with Antipholus and Dromio of Ephesus, and she says, "Most mighty duke, behold a man much wronged." (5.1.332). Recognition, *anagnorisis*, occurs as Adriana immediately interjects: "I see two husbands, or mine eyes deceive me" (5.1.333).

▲ The 2012 RSC production of *The Comedy of Errors*, with Bruce MacKinnon as Dromio of Syraceuse and Felix Hayes as Dromio of Ephesus.

The second comes a few lines later when the Abbess reveals herself as the wife of the hapless Egeon:

Whoever bound him, I will loose his bonds,
And gain a husband by his liberty. ...
O, if thou be'st the same Egeon, speak,
And speak to the same Emilia. (5.1.341–2, 346–7)

It is from this play that the structure as a serviceable formula for Shakespeare's future romantic comedies develops. One aspect of *The Comedy of Errors* helps create that formula, although Shakespeare does something a little different with this play. *The Comedy of Errors* adheres to the neoclassical unities of time, place and action, setting the whole of the action within a single place, with a single plot taking place within a single day. In this, Shakespeare is expertly using a neoclassical formula for drama. Perhaps he needed to do so before developing the confidence or experience to create his own structure for romantic comedy. We may recall that T. S. Eliot, advising young poets on how to write free verse, told them first to learn how to write a sonnet.

Shakespeare returns to the neoclassical unities only once in his works, in *The Tempest* (1611). Over the centuries, some literary critics have found that his willingness to depart from the established structural conventions is something to criticize, and today critics may still be wary of those who are willing to trust the plays to work for themselves as living drama. The fact remains, however, that *The Comedy of Errors*, like the other plays, continues to draw audiences and to be a box-office success. For Shakespeare's plays to succeed in the theatre, he had to entertain his theatrical audience, not convince sages of the study of their literary worth, even though the embryo of future 'literary' appeal is present in this play. There is so much more: poet, playwright, entrepreneur, farceur, businessman, artist. It is a complex but successful mix that developed something which mattered to his original audience and that continues to matter today.

A Midsummer's Night's Dream (1595–6)

I know a bank where the wild thyme blows,
Where oxlips and the nodding violet grows,
Quite over-canopied with luscious woodbine,
With sweet musk-roses and with eglantine:

(2.1.254–7)

It is possible that *A Midsummer Night's Dream* was written as an aristocratic bridal play, but there is no evidence that it was and it would have been unusual to have a play rather than a masque at such a celebration. The idea has tempted some commentators in the past since it is set as a bridal celebration for the wedding of Theseus, the Duke of Athens, and Hippolyta, Queen of the Amazons. The opening line of a play often tells us much about what is to occur, and this play is no exception to that rule.

Theseus: *Now, fair Hippolyta, our nuptial hour*
Draws on apace. Four happy days bring in
Another moon: (1.1.1–3)

There are five key words here: 'Now', 'nuptial', 'hour', 'apace', 'moon'. What is to happen in this play is 'now' as they await the fast-approaching time of their wedding, for the appearance of a new moon will herald a new time and a different existence. In emphasizing night-time, and the substitution of one 'moon' for 'another', Shakespeare is inviting the audience to enter the world of sleep and dream where the time will pass quickly and where 'desire' will be diverted. Theseus is eager to experience the transformation from bachelor to married man. And he talks of 'four days' but the play's actual events will prove to be only 'two'. We start with an invitation into the world of dream that is to be a prominent characteristic of this magical comedy.

No sooner is this conversation completed with Theseus' promises of celebration with "pomp, with triumph and with revelling" (line 20) than Shakespeare introduces a problem that occurs in the institution of arranged marriages and is, in this instance, associated with the opposing forces of love and death. A father, Egeus, interrupts:

Full of vexation come I, with complaint
Against my child, my daughter Hermia. (lines 23–4)

We find that Hermia wishes to marry Lysander but her father wishes her to wed Demetrius. Classical allusions are present in their names referring to the fall of Troy but the key issue becomes Theseus' judgement: Hermia must marry the man her father chooses or else die or be a virgin in the service of the goddess Diana. Already a familiar romantic comic formula begins to structure the plot. The lovers remove themselves from the society where the problem has arisen to the 'wood', where they undergo a series of adventures relating to self-knowledge and the search for identity, before a resolution of the errors brings about multiple marriages. It is worth pointing out that the word 'wood' also means 'mad' in this context, suggesting that the lovers themselves may be in a state of 'madness', or the heightened awareness that in neo-Platonic philosophy was sometimes associated with 'being in love'.

It is a play littered with fairies and 'rude mechanicals' (workers) who, according to traditional literary critics, play an essential role in the development of the humour and the passage towards resolution and harmony at the conclusion of the play. Cultural materialists, however, offer an alternative perspective. James H. Kavanagh, for example, drawing on Althusser, argues that the play exposes "a set of pre-conscious image-concepts in which men and women see and experience, before they think about, their place within a given social formation, with its specific structure of class and gender relations"[7].

From a different critical perspective Jonathan Bate argues that the "Authority figures, representatives of the day world of political power, win little sympathy" in the play and he directs us towards the nature of the theatrical experience of the play itself. "Always a man of the theatre, Shakespeare lives in a world of illusion and make-believe that hits at deepest truths: he knows that his world is fundamentally sympathetic to those other counter-worlds which we call dream and magic"[8].

Politically committed accounts within a context of intellectual critical debate do raise important issues for modern sensibility in reading or seeing the drama. Historically, however, with this early play, as with *The Comedy of Errors*, Shakespeare was surely once again intent on developing his craft and promoting his business. Great poet and dramatist though he was, he was also making money for himself and the acting troupe to which he belonged. Literary criticism of whatever persuasion often clashes in its evaluative mode with the notion of a script commercially designed to bring in the crowd. The separation of text from performance, that is the hallmark of much criticism, can produce a conflict with the popularism of the performance itself. Indeed, a dominant socially orientated culture ruled by academia or an hegemony of the learned elite, no matter what political views they may espouse, needs to be treated with caution. That the academic may see within the play fundamental ideological or literary issues worthy of study is not proof of its success in the context of its primary objective. Popularism and the academy are uneasy bedfellows.

In this chapter we will consider *A Midsummer Night's Dream* in the context of the Shakespearean formula for comedy and relate the geographical and identity relocation within the narrative to psychological and theatrical experience. As we will discover, this implies with *A Midsummer Night's Dream* the inclusion of geographical and identity transformation within the process of the dream and its relationship with the experience of the spectator participating in the dramatic performance as a member of the audience, laughing, responding, empathizing.

In the opening scene we can see an example of theatrical activity implicit within but also outside the text. When Theseus advises Hermia that her "father should be as a god" and she should obey him or either "die the death or to abjure / Forever the society of men" Hippolyta remains silent. Theseus, however, is given an indicative line later that shows what her stage reaction is. As he and Hippolyta exit, he says "Come, my Hippolyta. What cheer, my love?" (1.1.124). In Adrian Noble's renowned 1994 RSC production, Lindsay Duncan's Hippolyta slapped Theseus's face as they departed.

A correspondence was immediately established between the Duke of Athens and the Queen of the Amazons and Oberon and Titania, King and Queen of the Fairies, who in the forest are quarrelling over Titania's possession of a changeling boy. It is not unusual in theatrical practice for the same actors to play Theseus and Oberon and Hippolyta and Titania, naturally suggesting a link between the two which is taken into the forest scenes. Certainly it is to the forest that all the lovers go, and it is also where the workers from the city go to rehearse their play for the performance before the duke and his bride on their wedding evening.

Self-knowledge and reconciliation for the lovers is brought about by a magic potion taken from a flower and applied to their eyes: this initiates a series of comic confusions, not dissimilar in structure from those of the earlier *The Comedy of Errors*, as the potion is incorrectly applied to the lovers' eyes by Puck, a sprite serving Oberon. The reconciliation of the Oberon–Titania quarrel is similarly achieved by a magic potion placed on Titania's eyes, making her fall in love with one of the workers, Bottom the weaver, who has been "translated" into an ass by the command of Oberon. In giving up the changeling boy, she is reconciled to Oberon and Bottom is restored to himself, but not before Titania has been humiliated by the experience with Bottom. In a play that deals with 'dreams', Bottom thinks that his liaison with Titania has been a dream, just as she thinks that she has had a nightmare.

All go back to the court, where the workers present their play to a reconciled audience of three couples – Theseus and Hippolyta, Hermia and Demetrius, and Lysander and Helena, while the threat to Hermia if she disobeys her father seems magically to have disappeared. The workers' play is the tragedy of

Pyramus and Thisbe, characters who, like Romeo and Juliet, die for each other's love. In the hands of the mechanicals, however, it becomes a comedy which at its completion is followed by a 'Bergomask dance' of festivity. As all depart the stage, first Puck, then Oberon, Titania and the fairies enter and "bless this place" with a fairy song and dance.

There can be little doubt, therefore, that this ending reinforces the values of an aristocratic male-dominated hierarchical society that exerts political and social power over its members. But this is a comedy brought to a close with an epilogue spoken to the audience by Puck, who hopes that no one has been offended by what they have seen, and that if they disapprove, the action should be dismissed as being but a dream.

There is an issue, however, about male dominance in this play since it is possible that it was performed before Elizabeth I, who was known both as the 'Virgin Queen' and the 'Faerie Queen'. If so, there was the possibility of her being insulted by Titania, Queen of the Fairies, having fallen in love with an ass, an animal renowned for its large genitalia. The epilogue is possibly an attempt at insurance so that the queen would not be insulted by anything which she had witnessed.

Shakespeare, like his contemporaries, had to be careful of the sensitivities surrounding the queen's decision not to marry. James Shapiro (*1599: A Year in the Life of William Shakespeare*) reminds us that even to discuss the issue carried the death penalty. Julia Briggs (*This Stage-Play World*) notes that representations of the queen needed to celebrate her virginity, her constancy and her marriage to the realm. In *A Midsummer Night's Dream*, we find both a deliberate distancing of Elizabeth I from Titania, yet in Act 2 Scene 1 the inclusion of a reference to her in the performance. It is a neatly crafted move by the dramatist. Oberon tells Puck that he once saw Cupid shooting an arrow at "a fair vestal thronèd by the west", i.e. the English queen:

> *Cupid all armed; a certain aim he took*
> *At a fair vestal thronèd by the west,*
> *And loosed his love-shaft smartly from his bow,*
> *As it should pierce a hundred thousand hearts.*
> *But I might see young Cupid's fiery shaft*
> *Quenched in the chaste beams of the wat'ry moon;*
> *And the imperial votress passèd on,*
> *In maiden meditation, fancy-free.* (2.1.160–7)

It is the magic potion that gives the play its impetus for reconciliation. It is an elixir of love brought about by Cupid but able to be dispensed because of the vestal virginity of the queen – "Quenched in the chaste beams of the wat'ry moon" – on the eyes of those to fall in love with the one who wakes them. In all of this the young playwright is clearly on an artistic tightrope, maintaining his balance by continually advocating that it shouldn't all be taken too seriously. To do so would be to follow the mechanicals in their concern that the 'realism' of the play they are rehearsing might frighten the ladies. It is a device which in itself is protective of Shakespeare and his own acting troupe. This is the young playwright, the poet in command of his art form, pleasing the audience with his confidence, through his dexterity in language, narrative and political tact.

The dream appears to have been a brave but effective theatrical metaphor to use but one that had been used previously by other Elizabethan dramatists, such as John Lyly. M. C. Bradbrook distinguishes between the 'theatre of icon', largely derived from medieval mystery play cycles, and the 'theatre of dream', which in England finds its origin in the ritualistic process of medieval country games and ceremonies, reflected, for example, in Chaucer's dream poetry. Bradbrook held that the dream-like vision presented in such poetry developed an "interior drama ... of sentiment and feeling rather than of history", in which the dreams "constituted a special kind of fantastic 'game'"[9]. Although this exposed a concept of history which made her ideas vulnerable to criticism later by historicists and cultural materialists, she elucidated the power of traditional themes, games and structures on which Shakespeare drew in order to produce a play of the complexity of *A Midsummer Night's Dream*.

In the articulation of this convention, few literary or anthropological critics of the play have been more influential than C. L. Barber's *Shakespeare's Festive Comedy*. In this still important, though often challenged, work, Barber stripped away a sentimental concept of the play as Shakespeare's attempt to incorporate quaint folklore into his drama. Instead, he pointed to the complexity of the theatre/dream relationship, commenting:

> The whole night's action is presented as a release of shaping fantasy which brings clarification about the tricks of strong imagination. We watch a dream; but we are awake, thanks to pervasive humour about the tendency to take fantasy literally, whether in love, in superstition, or in Bottom's mechanical dramatics[10].

Later he draws a parallel between drama and exorcism: "dramatic art can provide a civilized equivalent for exorcism" not just through the conclusion of the play but through "the whole dramatic action, as it keeps moving through release to clarification"[11].

His views cannot be discounted; even in *Alternative Shakespeares*, Catherine Belsey, echoing Congreve, notes that "the plays are more than their endings"[12] and drawing on Derrida earlier reminds us that "meaning depends on difference, and the fixing of meanings is the fixing of difference as opposition"[13]. In the Christian tradition, exorcism is the purging of rooted opposition within an individual. We are, however, dealing with plays, artistic constructs created originally in the writing of the text by the dramatist, often drawing on known sources. As we noted with *The Comedy of Errors*, one such source is the Bible. In the Introduction to the Signet edition of that play, Harry Levin comments that the exorcists in the Acts of the Apostles can be 'exorcized' and argues that "the customary rhetorical questions of comedy ... become questions of existential bewilderment or expressions of cosmic vertigo: Do I dream or wake? Do we see double? Is he drunk or sober? Is she a liar or a fool? Who is crazy? Who is sane?"[14] The comedy cuts away at the foundations of what the characters and we perceive to be reality, questioning the very notions of perception and, indeed, of common experience. They can purge, they can exorcize.

Nowhere is this more the case than in *A Midsummer Night's Dream*, where drama is embodied in the metaphor of the dream, and the concept of the dream becomes a metaphor for the drama. Self-referential action draws attention through the play within a play to the artifice of what is being experienced not only by the fictitious characters but also by the audience watching the performance. Multi-layering takes place in relation to the marriage ritual and the notion of a celebratory play and to the constant references to the activity of dreaming. There is an added dimension of correspondence if the same actors are doubling parts such as Theseus/Oberon and Hippolyta/Titania or lesser roles involving the courtiers and the fairies. This is common in contemporary Shakespearean production and can be seen, for example, in Adrian Noble's 1994 RSC interpretation of the play.

William Empson, in *Some Versions of Pastoral*, explains the powerful concept of correspondence in dream artefact, telling us that "the power of suggestion is the strength of the double-plot; once you take two parts to correspond, any character may take on *mana* because he seems to cause what he corresponds to or be Logos of what he symbolizes"[15].

If this is the case with what is occurring on stage, is there not in the constant referential style and exposure of correspondence, a connection also with the audience, including not only the queen and courtiers in Shakespeare's day but every audience that experiences a performance. The spectators are people who are being invited by participation in the work also to define themselves by their perception of how the characters perceive correspondences and multi-layered realities through "parted" eyes. Puck and the fairies in this respect are not merely prompting the plot along, but are revealing the emotional, intellectual and social contradictions of people falling in love, marrying for status, pleasing their 'betters', being submissive by earning praise and profit, which are all experiences in life. Everything in comedy is fair game for humour, for the potion administered to the eyelids that blurs reality allows you, for example, to fall in love with an ass and thus become an ass yourself.

Discussing *The Comedy of Errors*, Harry Levin helpfully points us in the direction of Bergson's famous 'Essay on Laughter', "A situation is invariably comic", Bergson explains, "when it belongs simultaneously to two independent series of events, and is capable of being interpreted in two entirely different meanings at the same time." The complexity and multi-layering evident in *The Comedy of Errors* becomes more challenging within the complexity of the tightly knit narrative relationships of *A Midsummer Night's Dream*, referencing a further layer of correspondence both on the stage and into the auditorium. In this the dream metaphor facilitates an absurdly logical process that produces incongruity and a vision of the grotesque – Bottom as an ass. Conventional roles deal with the inner aspects of the human spirit and communicate them emphatically through the action and language of the play. Barber refers to Freud's claim that to indulge dreamlike irrationally with impunity is predominantly one of the basic satisfactions of wit[16]. This may be how the play works to expose ideologies and to engage emotional empathies that are tempered by the consciousness of the historical or current audience experience. So it is that in Act 2 Scene 2 Hermia awakes from a hateful dream which mirrors the actuality of her predicament:

Help me, Lysander, help me; do thy best
To pluck this crawling serpent from my breast!
Ay me for pity; what a dream was here?
Lysander, look how I do quake with fear:
Methought a serpent ate my heart away,
And you sat smiling at his cruel prey. (2.2.145–50)

Similarly, Titania's 'awakening' after the magic potion has been applied is one which resembles a dream-like illusion, that reality turns into a 'hateful' nightmare, that from another point of view can offer the fantasy that will allow the translation of Bottom the weaver into an ass. As Bottom is later to say, when the spell is removed and as he looks around for his friends:

… God's my life, stolen hence and left me asleep! I have had a most rare vision. I had a dream past the wit of man to say what dream it was. Man is but an ass, if he go about to expound this dream. Methought I was – there is no man can tell what. Methought I was – and methought I had – but man is but a patched fool if he will offer to say what methought I had. (4.1.197–201)

Of course, as an actor, the man playing the role of Bottom is a professional clown, a paid 'patched fool', but actually, who is not a 'patched fool' when they are seeking a sexual partner or a different status in a

▲ A 1974 production of *A Midsummer Night's Dream* with Linda Thorson as Titania and Nicky Henson as Bottom.

tightly controlled social order? So the awakening young lovers themselves point out that they are seeing things as indistinguishable, even as doubles, referring to the "parted eye":

Demetrius: *These things seem small and undistinguishable,*
Like far-off mountains turnèd into clouds.

Hermia: *Methinks I see these things with parted eye,*
When everything seems double. (4.1.180–3)

The nature of the perception of reality has been brought in and out of focus by the search for identity in the forest, resulting in an implied, although not certain, sustainability of relationships in the context of marriage. All has become a confusion, not just in the simple context of two sets of twins being mistaken with the obvious consequences as in *The Comedy of Errors*, but metaphysically with differing sets of lovers trying to make sense of who they are and who they love, where love is sometimes thought to be a form of 'divine' madness. This applies to Theseus and Hippolyta, Oberon and Titania, Demetrius and Helena, Lysander and Hermia, and even, within the mechanicals' play, Pyramus and Thisbe. Perceptual illusion can be tragic or comic or a mixture of both. Bottom exposes its distortions by linguistically parodying a Biblical passage. St Paul's first letter to the Corinthians says: "What no eye has seen, nor ear heard, nor the heart of man conceived, what God has prepared for those who love him" (1 Corinthians 2.9). Bottom, awakening, reflects:

> ... The eye of man hath not heard, the ear of man hath not seen, man's hand is not able to taste, his tongue to conceive, nor his heart to report, what my dream was. I will get Peter Quince to write a ballad of this dream: it shall be called 'Bottom's Dream', because it hath no bottom: (4.1.201–6)

As Malcolm Evans writes, "It is as if 'natural' language had taken an afternoon nap and woken to find that the bottom had fallen out of its world and the world out of its bottom"[17]! The weaver, Bottom, ironically is a man of 'endings', of 'conclusions' and 'effects'. He wants to play every part in the play, "Let me play the lion too" (1.2.53). But he is genuine in wanting to make what he does "more generous". He is a man who, despite his dream, has a sense of his identity and place in the society. In common aspiration, his is a simple acknowledgement of the dignity of an individual reminiscent of Costard's defence of Sir Nathaniel as "a marvellous good neighbour" in *Love's Labour's Lost* (5.2.599–600). If perspectives are to be found in the multi-layered texture of the play, then the character of Bottom is more genuine than most in his energy and enthusiasm for 'living' but, of course, he is a fiction and therefore not alive except in the actor portraying him.

That is not to deny, however, that within the dream framework Bottom needs to be seen also as a portrayal of subliminal bestiality in the sexual attitudes of human beings to each other. Peter Brook's landmark 1970 production was one of the most renowned 20th-century stagings of the work, giving a further impetus to the power of contemporary performance realization of an historical text. Its influence on Shakespearean production has continued to the present day. Brook was later to say that the effectiveness of the production depended on the "rough magic" implicit in the Shakespearean text. Set in a white box with a trapeze above, the lovers ran aimlessly about through one door and another and under the stilts of the circus fairies, taunted by Puck. Modern production was consciously invoking another arena of perceptual distortions – the circus – where wild animals are tame and clowns are kings.

There was a strong emphasis in the production on the sexuality of the play. The ass's phallus was emphasized by a fairy's arm erect between Bottom's legs, which caused some prurient concern at the time. But the bestial sexuality of the ass with Titania, the possessive conflict over the Indian boy between the fairy king and queen and the cruelties of the action were permitted to occur as they are in the play, without guilt or blame. This was the magic of the dream, of the unconscious self being made actual and thereby confronting the audience in their own conscious and unconscious realities. For the end of the play in the Brook production, there was a suggestion that the actors might all appear naked in their innocence but this would be to go too far in destroying the illusion by the affirmation of a particular, material reality. Rather, the production had to be comprehended in the context of the "parted eye" of the illusion coming to an end. The actors wore the purity of white, perhaps offering the cleansing of the psychological conflicts, signalling the ending of the play in which they mingled with members of the audience.

A Midsummer Night's Dream is an extraordinary work, allowing the geographical relocation of the characters into a magical forest to delve into the depths of psychological layers of perceptions of the self and others. In its historical context it exposes societal norms but in modern performance it similarly reveals, through humour, human behaviour and conditions which confront, expose and confirm the vagaries and fantasy of perceptions through the medium of the dream-like quality of theatre itself. In the prologue to John Lyly's play *Sappho and Phao* (1584), Shakespeare's fellow dramatist excused any offences that the work might produce by entreating the queen to imagine herself at the conclusion to have been in "a deep dream". As the fairies in *A Midsummer Night's Dream* bless the palace, Puck turns to the audience and asks for a similar understanding:

> *If we shadows have offended,*
> *Think but this, and all is mended,*
> *That you have but slumbered here*
> *While these visions did appear.* (5.1.393–6)

The dream is the metaphor of Shakespeare's theatre. It is the double vision that allows us to watch, listen, consider, correspond and reflect but rarely, if ever, to blame. This is its power in performance and its endurance. *A Midsummer's Night's Dream* continues to live in theatres around the world.

4

As You Like It
(1599–1600)

I can live no longer by thinking.

(5.2.35)

Some recent critics have termed *As You Like It* a 'greenworld' play, linking it particularly with *A Midsummer Night's Dream*. Such categorization appears to be related to plot rather than structure, the 'greenworld' plays being ones where the lovers make their way into a forest where they find their identities before returning to urban life. Like the RSC's 2012 season of 'shipwreck' plays (*The Comedy of Errors*, *Twelfth Night* and *The Tempest*), plot categorizations in the theatre may be for sound commercial reasons, or in education perhaps an aide memoire or a shorthand. But where does 'greenworld' start or end? Is *The Merry Wives of Windsor* a greenworld play since at its conclusion Falstaff is tricked into a forest? Or is *The Winter's Tale* a greenworld because Perdita is brought up in the countryside where Florizel, who is nurtured at court, woos her?

Over-categorization can be disadvantageous, yet for the past 60 years or so in particular people have felt comfortable putting creative works into categories. The 'Angry Young Men', the 'Theatre of Cruelty', the 'Theatre of the Absurd' are examples used by theatre critics to describe certain trends in 20th-century literature of theatre. The same is so for literary criticism: New Criticism, Formalism, New Historicism, Cultural Materialism are but a few of the labels used to describe certain critical practices. Possibly it has always been the case; Shakespeare ridicules the courtier Polonius in *Hamlet* for being too rhetorical in categorizing the types of plays the actors perform (2.2.351–5).

With *As You Like It* it is useful to begin an enquiry with its name. This is a play to be performed as you, the audience, like it. Such an interpretation of the title may demonstrate an expectation of a box-office certainty in the theatre. 'Come and see this play because it is as you like it'. But could there be a secondary subtextual interpretation? This is a play which has been written as you like it but with which I, the dramatist, may not be so enamoured. It is *as you like it* but not me. I have argued elsewhere[18] that Shakespeare may have written as the audience liked it but that through historical circumstances which we can only guess at, he may have been satiric in his choice of title. The play was written at a difficult time both for Shakespeare and his company:

> *Shakespeare's son had died, Burbage (the father of the theatre company) had died, the Company was facing financial risks, theatrical London was highly competitive and there were local professional difficulties with a popular actor (Will Kempe) …. So we have a play called As You Like It. But what if there is satire in this title? 'This is the play as you like it because as a dramatist I am having to write according to audience demands.' 'What if' thus allows us to create a challenge from the subtext of the play. It is a matter for us to decide[19].*

Such interpretations are, of course, speculative but there are historical issues behind the title which we might like to consider. Between 1599 and 1602 Shakespeare wrote some starkly contrasting plays: *Hamlet*, a tragedy of procrastinated revenge; *Troilus and Cressida*, a bitter war-torn drama exposing some of the worst traits of human psyche and conduct, and ending with a statement from Pandarus that he is bequeathing his venereal disease to the audience. Probably in between these two plays, or just before *Troilus*, is this romantic comedy, written according to a structural formula that the dramatist had established previously, in which a boy actor plays the part of a girl (Rosalind) who disguises herself as a boy (Ganymede), and as a boy plays a game of wooing the man with whom, as a woman, she has fallen in love (Orlando).

The plot theme of stories such as *As You Like It* could be argued to be ones of a certain titillation; boy actors playing the parts of girls dressed as boys going through a love ritual with men. The key to this type of interpretation is that the original actors of the female roles were young men. There must have been at least a certain, however limited, degree of homoeroticism in the performances historically, permitted within the law, which did not allow women to perform. This may have been heightened by location; as Puritan civic authorities would not permit theatres to be built within their London confines, public theatres were located either to the north of the city, where The Theatre was situated, or on the south bank of the Thames, in the brothel district, where Shakespeare's theatre was sited. The Globe, therefore, was in an erotic environment where it competed with other forms of entertainment, such as bear-baiting and cock-fighting.

Linked to the possible homoeroticism, we have further characters playing roles or scenes which add a further box-office appeal. The first is the sibling rivalry between Orlando and his cruel brother Oliver; at the beginning of the play this leads to the wrestling match watched by the ladies in which Charles the professional wrestler has been encouraged by Oliver to kill Orlando. So there is a good wrestling match, which is an entertainment in itself although contained within the narrative of the drama; in modern productions it is not unknown for professional wrestlers to be engaged for the role of Charles in order to improve the entertainment value of the scene. There is a parallel sibling rivalry plot as part of the play's political dimension, in which Duke Senior has been usurped by the current Duke Frederick and has had to resort with his courtiers to the 'greenworld' of the Forest of Arden, where he lives like 'Robin Hood'. There also Orlando flees with his old family servant, Adam, who on entering the greenworld nearly dies of exhaustion and starvation.

The greenworld itself is therefore no paradise but a rather wild place where the inhabitants hunt for food and where, towards the end of the play (4.3.96f), Orlando is wounded while rescuing his brother Oliver from a lioness. The shepherds Corin and Silvius add another layer of realism to the forest setting since they are what we would call tenant farmers, exposed to the harshness of the elements and to the inconsiderate behaviour of their absent exployer. The life of Robin Hood is not portrayed as particularly idyllic but rather is an experience of some danger and disquiet in what can be seen as a hostile environment. Yet even without the aid of a king or queen of the fairies as in *A Midsummer Night's Dream*, the Forest of Arden gives the impression of an enchanted wood, a wandering wood in which the characters have to come to terms with themselves and find their identities, as if they are in some kind of a denial of what has happened to them. Duke Senior attempts to justify his new existence:

Now, my co-mates and brothers in exile,
Hath not old custom made this life more sweet
Than that of painted pomp? Are not these woods
More free from peril than the envious court?
Here feel we not the penalty of Adam,
The seasons' difference, as the icy fang
And churlish chiding of the winter's wind,
Which, when it bites and blows upon my body,
Even till I shrink with cold, I smile and say
'This is no flattery: these are counsellors
That feelingly persuade me what I am'. (2.1.1–11)

Duke Senior complains that the old customs are being obscured by the bureaucratic needs of a society that is drifting away from the rhythms of the natural world. However, the duke's implied criticism of the behaviour that has resulted in the usurpation of his dukedom reveals that his only solution is to transplant the old social structure into the forest. There the old hierarchy of the court persists, along with some of its tensions. The courtier Amiens, in replying to the duke's sentiments, reveals the old customary, courtly obsequy:

I would not change it. Happy is your grace
That can translate the stubborness of fortune
Into so quiet and so sweet a style. (2.1.18–20)

Throughout, the traditional hierarchical social layering within this greenworld continues to mirror the social order in the world that has been left behind. This is demonstrated particularly by the different lovers, Celia and Oliver, Rosalind and Orlando in the upper strata and Phoebe and Silvius, Audrey and Touchstone in the lower. It is their existence at the lower end of society that allows Touchstone the clown to use his urbane knowledge of court behaviour to displace William in love, reducing him to the status of a 'clown':

Touchstone: *[I am] He, sir, that must marry this woman: therefore, you clown, abandon – which is in the vulgar 'leave' – the society – which in the boorish is 'company' – of this female – which in the common is 'woman', which together is: abandon the society of this female, or, clown, thou perishest .* (5.1.37–40)

Touchstone here assumes a ridiculous linguistic superiority to William, humorously placing himself in a dominant hierarchical position, allying himself in his imagination with a cultural and political superiority. He has found someone, William, whom he can force to relieve him of his position of 'clown', thereby allowing himself to move up the social ladder. In reality, however, he does not progress far since for him marriage is reduced to a means for legitimizing sexual activity: "Come, sweet Audrey: / We must be married, or we must live in bawdry" (3.3.61–2).

For her part, Phoebe falls in love with Rosalind disguised as Ganymede, who is of a higher social status, but in being a woman adds a further dimension to the sexual interest: two boy actors playing women, one of whom has disguised herself as a man. So a woman has fallen in love with a woman but as a boy and so the prospect of male/male theatrical eroticism is maintained.

In the midst of this sexual and social melée is the malcontent, Jaques. The pun on 'jakes' (privy) is within his name. Throughout the drama, Jaques demonstrates that he cannot be assimilated into the illusion that the characters are creating for themselves, since he feels compelled to defy their dream by reminding everyone of the frailty of flesh. His vision of a fallen, post-lapsarian world is in conflict with Duke Senior's Edenic vision. Jaques offers his own vision of human progress in the famous seven ages of man speech, in which he draws the parallel between life and the stage:

> *All the world's a stage,*
> *And all the men and women merely players;*
> *They have their exits and their entrances,*
> *And one man in his time plays many parts,*
> *His acts being seven ages.* (2.7.142f)

He continues by drawing out the different phases of human life moving towards imbecility and death, the end to which every individual is journeying from the moment of birth. Society is constant only in its repetition of the mutability of its members as each child is conceived and born. The process of living is also part of a process of dying, and death is the inevitable end of all human life. In this context, narrative plot built on the Shakespearean formulaic structure is a parable of a couple's mating game in a world of birth, copulation and death, where rebirth and an investment in youth is Nature's way of compensating for the rise and fall of the ever-ageing individual. This is something that the King of Navarre in the earlier play *Love's Labours Lost* fails to understand, and that the play labours to correct. As in *Twelfth Night*, Shakespeare draws out a parallel between the lovers searching for their sexual partners and the hunting of the wild deer, which was known for its sexual strutting. In Act 4 Scene 2, Jaques suggests that the deer's horns be presented to the duke as "a branch of victory", but the wearing of horns on the head was actually the sign of a cuckold, which, politically rather than sexually, Duke Senior has become through his loss of power. In this play as elsewhere, the relationship between sexual conquest, the hunt, political realities and the mutability of man is an echoing refrain.

The journey into the wood that is both Eden and the fallen world is a journey of discovery of the fragility of life itself, its vulnerability, transience and mutability. It is the essential understanding of "that is" that Feste notes also in *Twelfth Night*. Dressing up as the parson, the Fool remarks to Sir Toby:

> *For, as the old hermit of Prague that never saw pen and ink very wittily said to a niece of King Gorboduc, 'That that is, is.' So I, being Master Parson, am Master Parson; for what is 'that' but 'that', and 'is' but 'is'?* (*Twelfth Night*, 4.2.9–11)

Malcolm Evans finds such tautology problematic: "Any attempt to affirm something solid and transcendent, ultimately beyond language, by pinning one signifier to another, supposedly identical with itself, is heading for trouble."[20] So he finds the same problem with Touchstone's statement:

The heathen philosopher, when he had a desire to eat a grape, would open his lips when he put it into his mouth, meaning thereby that grapes were made to eat and lips to open. (5.1.25–7)

For Evans, this passage, like the tautology "truth is truth", is emblematic of the whole play and its festive conclusion in marriage. But such an argument depends upon looking at the play as if it is a philosophical thesis. It is a play in which Fools talk nonsense and indulge in tautology. It is a drama in which narrative follows structure to an ending which does not encompass all but which will bring the story to a satisfactory close that is as artificial as the play itself.

As with *A Midsummer Night's Dream*, Shakespeare works at his dramatic endeavours, reflects upon them and in doing so develops theatre itself as a metaphor. The underlying structural formula which allows the plot to function and resolve itself in a recognition scene is a self-referential construct. In *As You Like It*, it is highly contrived by Rosalind, who promises a satisfying resolution to all the problems and misconceptions which, to some extent, she has brought about by dressing as Ganymede to lead Celia and Touchstone into the forest.

The choice of the name Ganymede (in Roman mythology, Jove's cupbearer) demonstrates Rosalind's fictional confidence to construct events as she pleases. But there are also literary homosexual references in the name which may have been recognized by some, if not all, of the audience. There has been throughout the narrative a homoerotic teasing in the conduct of her love game with Orlando. That has to be brought fictionally to an impasse when the boy (actual) acting as a girl dressed as a boy can no longer satisfy his/her lover. Teasing and pretending are not enough. In Act 5 Scene 2 line 35, Orlando declares "I can live no longer by thinking" and Rosalind replies, "I will weary you then no longer with idle talking." Their playing must come to an end but the play itself, as with their 'playing', has also to be concluded within the larger context of the overall fiction.

▲ A 2009 production of *As You Like It*, with Rosalind, disguised as Ganymede (Katy Stephens), and Orlando (Jonjo O'Neill), watched by Celia (Mariah Gale), in the Forest of Arden.

In Shakespeare's sonnet sequence, the attraction to the male patron is transmuted into a heterosexual competitive three-way relationship, with the dark lady's presence prompting the dark thoughts of sexual unease in the poet. Here, in 'as you, the audience, like it', a similar hiatus in the sexual journey takes place. There has to be more in the relationship than the fiction of being in love. The actuality, homosexual or heterosexual, of physical consummation needs to be evidenced through the laws of the drama which are being dictated by the underlying structure of the plot itself, and by a particular commitment to the institution of marriage. The dramatic conclusion of the play metaphorically reinforces the institution of marriage which, like a play, is a ceremonial public act.

Rosalind has to reveal herself and does so through the artificial agency of the masque, assisted by the god Hymen, who reveals her in her woman's attire although 'she' is still, of course, being played by a boy actor. Daughter is reunited with father and with the lover whom she has wooed in her male attire. Phoebe realizes her mistake in falling for a woman dressed as a boy. Touchstone has his way to sexual satisfaction with Audrey, and so the fiction concludes with a representation of the various levels of human behaviour that exist within marriage itself.

But there remain many unanswered questions. What about the rival dukes? Whilst a means has been found to bring Oliver into the wood and for him to fall in love with Celia, a device outside the harmony of the structural formula has to be created by the dramatist to allow a reconciliation between the two dukes. As discussed in the Introduction, with little prior reference, Orlando and Oliver are given a brother hitherto largely forgotten (by the audience), who appears on stage for the first time to state that he is the second son of Sir Rowland, a solution so outrageous that it causes the audience to laugh and to forgive the dramatist for this implausibility in the illusion of the play. Other issues nevertheless are brought to the fore. The artifice of the second son's appearance draws attention to the construct of the play as much as, if not more so than, Hymen's masque. Its artificiality proclaims the self-referential nature of the artefact, alleviating the implausibility of the usurping Duke Frederick's meeting with a holy man and subsequent departure to a monastery.

The device allows also for a reconciliation of the Jaques position since he has been left isolated by the plot. As the outsider he still needs a narrative solution. The dramatist has him follow Duke Frederick's fortunes now as before he had followed Duke Senior in his banishment, possibly because he symbolizes in his name the detritus which he is unable to forget, and that makes him unfit for human, urbane society. The fiction appears to reveal that wherever you go, your avowed commentary on what you are, your understanding of your illusion in the comprehension of your being, will follow you, determining the consistency of your individual actions and place in society. Shakespeare, however, adds one more twist.

As the play tries to escape from the confines of its self-imposed artificiality it suddenly violates the requirements of the comic structure itself. Rosalind appears as the epilogue. Who now is this character? She addresses the audience as a woman but the reality is that she is still the boy actor, who remains in his female role as he addresses the audience even though the play is over:

It is not the fashion to see the lady the epilogue, but it is no more unhandsome than to see the lord the prologue. If it be true that good wine needs no bush, 'tis true that a good play needs no epilogue ... If I were a woman, I would kiss as many of you as had beards that pleased me, complexions that liked me and breaths that I defied not. (5.4.173–5, 183–5)

What do we have here but a resonance of the sexual teasing that has pervaded the whole? Gender identity is a referent of self-awareness, whether in the case of male, female or transsexual. Consequently the sexual ambiguities remain in the closing of the play as an invitation to reflect further on what has been experienced: the bridge between the presence of the audience as an audience, the actor as a boy and the fiction that has been enjoyed. In the conclusion we are presented with a final affirmation of the artificiality of the theatre, reflecting the humour of ambiguous sexuality for the pleasure of all, freed from the structured confines of the law, replicated in the structure of the play itself and that, teasingly, remains in the fictitious world. After such an epilogue there is, for now, no more to be said. The laws of correspondence between what is portrayed and those that portray and those who, as members of the audience, are participants in the portrayal remain within the memory of the dramatic experience which was the process of the play. The audience has had to live by thinking, by imagining but now it is over. This is as you like it. Whether this is as the dramatist liked it is probably an irrelevance about which we can only speculate but the epilogue confirms his certainty and confidence that the tease, the play, was as his audience liked it.

Twelfth Night or What You Will (1601)

Do I stand there?

(5.1.211)

Noting the death of Shakespeare's son, Hamnet, in 1596, Jonathan Bate writes,

> *Though we should always be wary of inferring authorial autobiography from the words of fictional characters in a play, there is an inescapable poignancy to the images of loss in* Twelfth Night: *when Feste sings of sad cypress ... or Viola alludes to a funeral monument, it is tempting to think of Shakespeare's own lost boy*[21].

In other art forms, however, most notably paintings, it is almost a critical commonplace to draw biographical relationships from the artefacts themselves. Van Gogh's mental state was evidenced through the contrast of bright and dark colours or through the way he appeared to see the world; Picasso's blue period following the death of an intimate male friend; El Greco's defective sight producing his elongated style. Shakespeare had twins, a girl, Judith, and a boy, Hamnet. In August 1596 Hamnet died, aged 11 years. We do not know how Shakespeare took the news; we can only speculate. How did he cope with it? Was he in Stratford when his son died or was he in London? We do not know, but about four years later he was to write *Hamlet*, a play of multiple deaths which, as Peter Davison anecdotally notes, may have another personal reminiscence in the context of Ophelia's death:

> *Shakespeare may have been prompted to the mode of Ophelia's death by an incident that occurred near Stratford when Shakespeare was fifteen. A young woman slipped into the River Avon when going*

for a pail of water and drowned. Her name was Katherine Hamlett[22].

Such questions of influence are obviously speculative at a distance of over 400 years but are nevertheless provocatively intriguing. Shakespeare happened to have twins, and the concept of twins did become structurally important within his comedies. In *The Comedy of Errors*, there are two sets of twins. *A Midsummer Night's Dream* has two sets of couples of which the two boys can hardly be distinguished from each other except by reference to the women they purport to love (and who are often dressed almost identically in modern productions). In *As You Like It*, we are presented with two girls and two brothers at the centre of a romantic comedy. It is possible that Shakespeare's own personal experience drew him towards thinking about 'pairs' and 'twins' as a basic element of dramatic structure, although we cannot be sure of how conscious he was of the implications of making this choice.

In 1601, Shakespeare returns explicitly to the portrayal of twins, girl and boy, Viola and Sebastian. Viola survives a shipwreck but fears her brother is drowned. Her brother survives the shipwreck but fears his sister is drowned. Shakespeare has returned to the plot territory of *The Comedy of Errors*, but with a difference. It may be to do with his growth in maturity as a dramatist, but surely we have to note that probably between the writing of *The Comedy of Errors* and *Twelfth Night* Hamnet has died. Death is present throughout the play, not just as a framing device – as in *The Comedy of Errors*, where Egeon is sentenced to death unless he can find redemption within the hours of daylight – but permeating the fabric of the play with a gentle melancholy, as exemplified by the Fool's song:

Come away, come away, death,
And in sad cypress let me be laid.
Fly away, fly away, breath,
I am slain by a fair cruel maid.
My shroud of white, stuck all with yew,
O, prepare it!
My part of death, no one so true
Did share it. (2.4.53–60)

The *carpe diem* ('seize the day') motif represents a balance between the energy of life and the finality of death, which can strike at any time.

The play's title, *Twelfth Night, or What You Will*, has attracted the attention of scholars over the years. The 20th-century critic C. L. Barber linked *Twelfth Night*, as he did *A Midsummer Night's Dream* and other comedies, with festive traditions. He observes, "The title tells us that the play is like holiday misrule – though not just like it, for it adds 'or what you will'."[23] More recently, Barber's views, although still respected, have been challenged, particularly by New Historicist critic Stephen Greenblatt. He questions Barber's claim that in the play there is a "basic security" which "explains why there is so little that is queazy in all Shakespeare's handling of boy actors playing women, and playing women pretending to be men"[24]. Such a critical position raises Greenblatt's ire, prompting him to call for a different kind of reading: "how can we unsettle the secure relation between the normal and the aberrant? How can we question the nature that like a weighted bowl so providentially draws to her bias and resolves the comic predicaments? I propose ... [that] we must historicize Shakespearean sexual nature, restoring it to its relation of negotiation and exchange with other social discourses of the body"[25].

He continues by advocating that the play has to be considered not in isolation but by "swerving" into historical contextual narratives. He subsequently elaborates this view by extending his interesting research into historical medical transsexual accounts of the period. Although this is a somewhat strained, if not obscure, correspondence of interest in relation to the play itself, it nevertheless offers a critical corrective.

There is some validity in both viewpoints. Barber was writing at a time before the 'sexual revolution' of the last 50 years or so questioned the notion of "basic security" in assumptions, description, articulation or judgement of 'norms'. But Greenblatt's position isn't beyond question either. Kiernan Ryan, challenging the Greenblatt approach, suggests that we go back to the text itself as an active product in an historical process[26]. With *Twelfth Night* we may take this suggestion further by investigating the structural foundation that makes the play work dramatically. Shakespeare's structural formula in this play not only allows the development of a good story, as the audience likes it, but offers an even more complex depiction of character development, and also of emotion, social satire, sexual humour and ambiguity, whilst the audience is encouraged to make of it what you want or what you will. So the subtitle of the play is drawn to our attention.

Let us experiment, using 'what you will' in the context of 'what if'. Let's imagine a scenario in which a playwright, knowing his sources, which are various, and mapping out his play, asked himself: what if we have a duke who is infatuated with self-love and who professes love for a wealthy woman of a slightly lower social status than himself? What if that woman is in mourning for the death of her brother, just a year after the death of her father? What if she rejects him, just as Elizabeth I rejected Philip of Spain? What would he do? A man of self-love, let me call him Orsino – a foreign dignitary of that name had recently visited London – and given the attribution of that name, a young cub, how would he react?

But let me, Shakespeare, complicate it further. What if at the time of this rejection, a young woman is shipwrecked on his land, which I will call Illyria as it sounds like, but is not, Elysium (Heaven). What if she thinks her brother, who could be her twin, has drowned and gone to Elysium, but unknown to her has also survived. What would she do to survive in this strange land? What if we call the two women by similar names, making a connection between the two even in the letters of their name, providing in narrative parallels an element of a thematic relationship. The first could be Olivia, as in the olive tree, with its connection to the Christian tradition of sadness manifest in relation to the death of Christ. The second woman, the shipwrecked one, we call Viola, a violet being the pure flower of tranquillity, now saddened by death and believing herself to be in danger in an alien land.

▲ The opening of the 2012 RSC production of *Twelfth Night*, with Viola (Emily Taaffe) on the 'shore' in the foreground and Orsino (Jonathan McGuinness) behind.

By asking 'what if' we may develop an understanding not of the way Shakespeare actually created his play but of the narrative itself. At its centre there are two women who are both sad and in mourning, but whose names interact with each other, thus providing a correspondence between the two.

We can, of course, introduce further complications into this speculative model. What if there is another potential lover? Just as Olivia is not equal in status to Duke Orsino and rejects him, what if the chief steward of her household, not someone of her station, also believes that she can love him but, like the duke, is self-indulgent and self-delusional in his desire? Let him even have the letters of her name, Olivia, embedded within his own, 'Malvolio', but incongruous with it. He can be a

Puritan who manipulates her mourning in an attempt to become indispensable to her but is frustrated by her relations and members of her household who need to be the opposite: frivolous, easy-going, self-indulgent, fun-loving but possibly angry with life. One of these can be a visitor, a ridiculous figure also wanting to woo her but having no chance – Sir Andrew Aguecheek – who is being manipulated by her uncle, Sir Toby, an archetypal self-indulgent corpulent character, who is outwardly fun-loving but inwardly bitter.

These 'what ifs' provide a recipe for the conflict which is the ingredient of good drama. But a few more ingredients might also be included: a fool, who stands apart and yet simultaneously can engage with every level of the society that the play depicts, who comments on what he sees and yet willingly participates in the events. Shipwrecked Viola can dress in similar clothes to her apparently dead brother and call herself Cesario ('little Caesar'). Her brother can be named Sebastian, after the saint who, according to Christian tradition, was shot to death with arrows for his love of God. His name is a foil to that of the others: Toby, Malvolio and Toby's gull Sir Andrew Aguecheek, who in trying to profess his love to Olivia is not so much rejected as simply ignored. Sir Andrew can even be made to pick a fight with the girl pretending to be the man Cesario. The boy actors, feigning female reticence but pitted against a cowardly adversary, could make such an episode into farcical, appealing comedy.

Now we have the ingredients of the play. We start with the problem relating to death, indeed a number of deaths. We have a geographical relocation, in that Viola is washed up on a strange shore and, for her own protection, disguises herself as a man who gains service in Orsino's court. In the search for her own identity she tries to teach Orsino what love is, and in the process she falls in love with him. He, for his part, begins to depend on her, thinking her a man, and sends her to woo Olivia on his behalf. Olivia instantly falls in love with the cross-dressed Viola/ Cesario. Confusion reigns, the fool commentates, a trick is played on the other false lover, the Puritan Malvolio, by Sir Toby and the maid Maria, who, in the Catholic tradition, is named after Mary, the revered Mother of God. All struggle to find out who they really are. Sebastian the twin brother, meanwhile, is saved from the sea and, like Antipholus of Syracuse in *The Comedy of Errors*, is mistaken for his twin but this time it is a twin sister. In the errors of *Twelfth Night* and the topsy-turvy world that it depicts, humour and sadness, love and injustice, redemption and aggression may mingle.

All of these are resolved in the end by the exposure of all the errors in a single scene. Secretly, Olivia has persuaded Sebastian to marry her, thinking him to be Cesario. The duke himself now arrives to try to court Olivia, but this time in his own person. Cesario is with him and Olivia, thinking Cesario is a man, reveals she is married to Orsino's servant. He responds by turning on her and on Cesario with the violence of the adolescent young cub whose temperament his characterization has threatened to reveal throughout the play.

Meanwhile, Sebastian, named after an agent of true love, has fought with Sir Toby and now appears on stage at the same time as Viola. It is one of the great recognition scenes in Renaissance drama, a moment of quiet *anagnoris* is resolving the errors with an emotional power that affects audience and dramatic characters alike, as he sees his lost twin sister and asks, as the complexities and confusions melt away:

> *Do I stand there? I never had a brother,*
> *Nor can there be that deity in my nature*
> *Of here and everywhere. I had a sister,*
> *Whom the blind waves and surges have devoured.*
> *Of charity, what kin are you to me?*
> *What countryman? What name? What parentage?*

Viola replies simply:

> *Of Messaline. Sebastian was my father,*
> *Such a Sebastian was my brother too,*
> *So went he suited to his watery tomb ….*
> *If nothing lets to make us happy both*
> *But this my masculine usurped attire,*
> *Do not embrace me till each circumstance*
> *Of place, time, fortune, do cohere and jump*
> *That I am Viola …* (5.1.211–16, 217–19, 235–9)

Within this lengthy recognition scene, which the above quotation draws out a little, are the traditional elements of classical *anagnorisis*, including, for example, a physical identifier used to substantiate the characters' claims – "My father had a mole upon his brow. / And so had mine." (lines 228–9) – but there is also added a Christian reference of resurrection, though secularized. As the risen Christ forbids those who first see him from touching him, so here, unlike Rosalind in *As You Like It*, Viola instructs that she cannot be embraced until all has been finally confirmed. *Anagnorisis* is being gently fused with a secularized expression of the deepest Christian 'mystery', resurrection. The impact on the original audiences, consciously or unconsciously, must have been immense and, despite the greater secularization of our contemporary society, this conclusion still retains its emotional power.

So it is that the main narrative of the play is brought to a conclusion. Characterization, however, becomes central to the play. The mature Shakespearean plays, whether comedy or tragedy, insist on the statement of the identity of the self. In *Hamlet*, the prince, returning to Elsinore, reveals himself at the graveside of his love, Ophelia, "This is I, / Hamlet the Dane" (5.1.210–11). In the comedy of *Twelfth Night* the twin sister finding her brother leads her narrative to point to the statement of proof which will show that "I am Viola" (5.1.239). These statements of the substance of the name are confirmations of sanity, self-reconciliation and of community and knowledge. Yet how does the actor or actress playing the respective parts rehearse themselves into an understanding of the fictional character they are portraying?

They do so, of course, by their training, their technique and accomplishment in their profession. The directors in assisting them in any given performance usually try to find a 'through-line' for the play as a whole, a logic of interpretation that will provide a consistency in communication. For example, Sir Peter Hall, founding director of the Royal Shakespeare Company, summed up *Twelfth Night* for his famous 1958 production by telling his actors that the play "like all the comedies, is about growing up"[27]. It is a typical all-embracing, simple statement by a director who has to engage his cast with a dominant idea that will provide the glue, the consistency, that will cement the elements of the production together. For his 1970 production of *A Midsummer Night's Dream*, Peter Brook similarly held to the unifying idea of the play's "rough magic", a phrase coined by Shakespeare himself in *The Tempest*. As with Brook in 1970, Hall in 1958 felt he needed to break away from stereotypical productions, presenting a challenge to the cast and ultimately the audience. Hall writes of his *Twelfth Night*, which produced some "outrage" and "controversy":

> ... because I had rethought the interpretation of Olivia ... Traditionally , the character had always been portrayed as straight-laced and matronly. But the play is, among other things, about Olivia's tribulations in growing up. Geraldine [McEwan]'s Olivia was vain, a little ditsy, not to say silly. But she was nonetheless heartbreaking – a young girl suddenly thrust into being mistress of a big household[28].

So with Viola in John Barton's famous production 11 years later, where – quietly, softly, magically, with a cadence of joy in her throat – Judi Dench revealed her name, in what proved to be an almost Chekhovian interpretation of the play with its blend of outrage and subtlety. (See Stanley Wells' account of this production[29].)

As these examples show, characterization comes from the text but is created through the actor, who is a product of their own age, interpretating a centuries-old malleable text. Hall's or Barton's productions today would not hold the same force as they did in 1958 or 1969, largely because the tastes and expectations of modern audiences have changed.

The 2012 RSC production with Jonathan Slinger as Malvolio revealed a cruder, though equally effective, bawdier humour in a more explicitly dangerous environment in which Viola had literally come out of a reservoir of water. A director might advise the actor playing Malvolio that, whilst the characters of Viola and Olivia are experiencing the tribulations of youth, his character through harsh victimization is one that perhaps cannot learn by experience and it is that which a particular director may feel needs to be communicated to an audience. In the text, Malvolio is imprisoned, a Puritan being duped by a Saturnalian. But he is no less 'human' in characterization than the Saturnalian himself. Jonathan Slinger's bawdy exposure in the yellow stockings scene was reflective of a character 'caught out' by his own sexual desire – a comically modern Priapus. In the text, Sir Toby exercises his bitter revenge on Malvolio by manipulating the authority to which his own superior social status entitles him to destroy one of the servile, but aspiring, supporters of that order. Malvolio is depicted as one who believes in the superiority of the very social order that humiliates him. The steward's self-deception ironically has led him to misunderstand the cruel nature of society itself. "That, that is, is" (4.2.10) may be a tautology in the play but it is portrayed as a reality of conduct. One does not get above oneself in a hierarchical order of things and Malvolio's "I'll be revenged on the whole pack of you" (5.1.360) ludicrously shows that at the conclusion he is still delusional about himself. By being imprisoned he has been deliberately kept away from the recognition scene. However, in the final scene, Olivia goes as far as her society will allow in promising him that he can be "both the plaintiff and judge / Of thine own cause" (5.1.338–9). His humiliation is too great. Trevor Nunn's 1996 film version of the play sees him, luggage in hand, leaving the household for ever. It is a justifiable corollary to the text. In the end, Sir Toby conforms to the values of the society by marrying Maria and the Fool remains, just as Malvolio had accurately depicted him, an outsider within the household, an important parasitic commentator who can easily outlive his comic or nuisance value. The Fool knows it to be true but, unlike Malvolio, does not delude himself into thinking that he is other than what he is.

In his book *1599*, the historicist critic James Shapiro is, perhaps, unfairly dismissive of the quality of this play. He writes that "Twelfth Night was a time-tested and accomplished if somewhat formulaic throwback to earlier Shakespearean comedy – and it would be the last of this kind he would write."[30]. There is, however, both a looking back and an anticipation of the future in the 'shipwreck' plays. As we have seen, the farcical nonsense of Egeon's shipwreck story in *The Comedy of Errors* takes a different turn in the character complexities of *Twelfth Night*, where so many of the potential lovers "suffer a sea change / Into something rich and strange", a description found in *The Tempest* (1.2.464–5), written approximately ten years later.

In theatrical terms, *Twelfth Night* presents a merry-go-round of life, with people disguising themselves, their professions, their senses, their affections, their loves, their identities and their souls in order to protect themselves from the wind and the rain that Feste's final song emphasizes. In *Twelfth Night* there is no place for looking back – what is dead is gone – but the present still has to define itself according to the political and social forces, the demands of social and religious conformity, that control it, which leaves a modern audience with questions emanating from the nature of both structure and plot.

So what is the play's potential affinity with a 21st-century audience? Is it that the disguises that are adopted, the hypocrisy of the self-righteous, the indulgence of those who are delusionally self-gratifying and the cruelty of revenge still underpin society, or does the play signify nothing but words, thereby allowing us to reinforce our own sense of virtue or morality or love without being prompted to the challenge of change itself? Should we be confined to 'a ship of fools' as depicted in John Marston's *The Fawn*, a play written around the same time as *Twelfth Night*, or merely endure and accept the "rain that raineth every day"? We will never know how Shakespeare reacted as a father to the death of his son. Maybe it does or maybe it does not haunt this play. But behind this story something lingers. We are born, we cry, we laugh, we endure and we die either in youth or in old age. It is a view of life and humanity which *King Lear* is later to confirm. In this comedy, Shakespeare's play confronts both life and death, bringing characters 'back to life' to an Illyria where self-absorption finally gives way to a recognition of the mutuality of love. The dramatic structure of Shakespeare's play determines that this is so. We may ask whether he offers us a timeless or trans-historical cultural truth by offering hope in the very process of a self-recognition that gives way to love as the foundation of the social order. We may find critical help in understanding what he attempted to do by fictionalizing a 'what if', but in the end Shakespeare still leaves us to make of it 'what you will'.

The Taming of the Shrew (1592?)

Forward, I pray, since we have come so far,
And be it moon, or sun, or what you please.
An if you please to call it a rush-candle,
Henceforth I vow it shall be so for me.

(4.3.12–15)

In the late 20th century, there was much interest in *The Taming of the Shrew* in relation to the cultural and critical consciousness of the feminist movement. This play could be seen as having a direct relevance to the concerns of Feminism, and the critical and theatrical responses that it generated were sometimes provocative, although familiarity has to some extent ameliorated some of its more disturbing effects. In this chapter, I will:

▶ examine the relationship of *The Taming of the Shrew* with the early play *The Taming of A Shrew* to demonstrate how directorial choice and interpretation can resolve or avoid apparent sensitive problems

▶ refer to a number of complementary late 20th-century productions, some of which conflate the two plays

▶ consider how the structure and plot of *The Taming of the Shrew* works to allow an open-ended conclusion.

In 1594 a Quarto edition of a play entitled *The Taming of A Shrew* was published. There are similarities between this play and Shakespeare's *The Taming of the Shrew*. Editors are not certain, however, whether *The Taming of A Shrew* is an early quarto of the play on which Shakespeare later drew or simply one that appeared at the same time as *The Taming of the Shrew*, which was included in the First Folio of 1623. There were no copyright laws in Shakespeare's days. Plays were 'stolen' or 'copied', for example, by jobbing actors who moved from company to company, memorizing the plays as best they could, or by actors being 'poached' by rival companies for that purpose. On the whole, critics regard the First Folio as the only authoritative text, probably deriving from

Shakespeare's working papers ('foul papers') or from some other adaptation.

There is clearly a relationship between the two plays but its nature is generally considered to be a speculative question. H. J. Oliver, for the Oxford Shakespeare, gives an informative publication history of the two plays, noting the inevitability "that for hundreds of years *A Shrew* being the first of two versions ... to be published, and being clearly inferior, should have been assumed to be the first composed and to be, in whatever sense the source of the Folio play *The Shrew*." He goes on to state that it was not known if Shakespeare had anything to do with it but that it was generally accepted "that he had set out to improve upon it". Oliver details the debates about the relationship and notes the parallels between the two versions. The matter is probably a textual issue, but one that we do not have enough information to resolve satisfactorily. Maybe Shakespeare's version of the play was one of those that brought scorn on him as "an upstart crow" and contributed to the evidence of his having allegedly 'borrowed' other writers' ideas or scripts. Certainly later in his career he was a victim of such conduct by others. Whatever the relationship between the two versions of this play, the issue continues to fascinate critics and, perhaps more particularly, theatre directors, especially in the context of the framing play that is used to provide the dramatic structure of *A Shrew*.

This framing device is the story of a drunken tinker, Christopher Sly, being dressed up as an aristocrat and taken off to watch a play, creating thereby a play within the play. *The Taming of A Shrew* concludes with Sly being dressed again "in his own apparel" and left where he had earlier been found drunk. The Tapster wakes him, Sly asks:

> *... whats all the*
> *Plaiers gon: am not I a Lord?*

and continues:

> *... oh Lord sirra, I have had*
> *The bravest dream tonight, that ever thou*
> *Hardest in all thy life ...*
> *... I know now how to tame a shrew,*
> *I dreamt upon it all this night till now,*
> *And thou hast wakt me out of the best dreame*
>
> *That I ever had in my life, but Ile to my*
> *Wife presently and tame her too*
> *And if she anger me.*
> (Quarto 1594, *The Taming of A Shrew*[31]; typology slightly amended.)

This scene is omitted from the Folio script of *The Shrew* but it reminds us of Bottom's awakening in *A Midsummer Night's Dream* (4.2.195) and affirms the concept of the play as dream, and of the audience witnessing the play as a dream. H. J. Oliver, along with other critics, rejects the notion of the reintroduction of the Sly scenes to close off the Shakespearean play, noting: "One does not improve a farce by ending it with the reminder that it may have been only a farce; far better to let the audience make that judgement, if it wishes to make it."[32].

Oliver's comment aligns with that of Juliet Dusinberre. In not bringing the character of Sly back onto the stage, Shakespeare's *The Shrew* ends with Lucentio commenting on Petruchio's taming of Kate, with the words *"'Tis wonder, by your leave, she will be tamed so"* (5.1.201).

Dusinberre comments:

> *Shakespeare leaves the question open. To end the play with a return to the cornerstones of Christopher Sly's beggary would mean insisting that it was only illusion which gave birth to the vision of domestic order.*[33]

She argues that Sly in *The Taming of A Shrew* goes home "to face the music from his harridan wife", but in not bringing back Sly at the end and concluding instead with Lucentio's final sceptical words, Shakespeare generates an "ambiguity" in an "equivocal setting" so that "Kate's transformation is a miracle in the world where miracles happen, the theatre, where beggars are Lord".

Many modern directors, however, have followed the temptation of imposing the framing device from the conclusion of *A Shrew* onto *The Shrew* in performance. To start the play with it and then let it slip away, as happens in *The Shrew*, appears to them to be structurally incomplete. So questions are asked: as a master craftsman did Shakespeare actually fail to round off this early play? Did he really create a framing structure and then forget about it? Or did he take the start of the framing structure from an original play, *A Shrew*, but decide deliberately not to reintroduce it at the end? This is a rich area of speculation for literary critics and directors alike, where no one can be right or wrong. It is a matter of interpretation, and it is in interpretation that *The Taming of the Shrew* derives controversy and indeed energy in the contemporary world.

For modern sensibilities the play can pose many difficult questions. In particular they centre around the treatment of Kate and her reproach to the Widow in Act 5 Scene 1, where she says:

> *Thy husband is thy lord, thy life, thy keeper,*
> *Thy head, thy sovereign: one that cares for thee,*
> *And for thy maintenance, commits his body*
> *To painful labour both by sea and land,*
> *To watch the night in storms, the day in cold,*
> *Whilst thou liest warm at home, secure and safe,*
> *And craves no other tribute at thy hands*
> *But love, fair looks and true obedience;*
> *Too little payment for so great a debt.*
> *Such duty as the subject owes the prince*
> *Even such a woman oweth to her husband.* (5.1.158–68)

Jonathan Bate points out that this is not a generalized statement but is addressed to the Widow alone, but in adopting this view he demonstrates, to an extent, the apologetic interpretation critics and theatre directors adopt in their attempts to find solutions to a sensitive modern issue. Some productions have dressed Kate in sackcloth to make this statement, in order to indicate that she is a battered wife and that she is now compelled to justify the behaviour of her abuser.

Dusinberre and other feminist critics are less severe, allowing for a greater openness of interpretation.

Marilyn French, for example, notes that the ending of the play parodies the "suggestion that subordination, when volitional (chosen as an alternative to confusion, or learned, as internalized morality), can lead to joy, to true community and love in decorum"[34]. A social order exists, she argues, which necessitates Kate relinquishing "her chafing at subordination before the male can give up his oppressive power over her"[35].

According to these interpretations, Shakespeare actually reveals the social realities of his time, which can be glimpsed and appreciated through the ambiguities of the text itself. Modern interpretations that close off the text or that dress Kate in sackcloth to reveal her as a battered wife or that sentimentalize the action through imposing the concluding framing structure, may allow the audience to leave the theatre without fully appreciating the challenge of the play's process. In revealing social order and the need for conformity to it, issues relating to social order itself are naturally raised by Shakespeare but to what dramatic purpose or effect. John Drakakis, in correspondence with me, comments: "Either the play is 'conservative' in supporting the existing order or it allows an audience to glimpse critically the nature of the order and the anxieties that it produces. If aesthetically the ending justifies the social order, then it justifies Kate's inferiority. If it questions it (the ironical reading) then it is critical of an order that will allow a husband to subdue a wife." There is, he notes, a third way, which is that "Kate is very cunning and fakes it, knowing what her husband wants and pretending to oblige". So we have at least three possible interpretations that can be followed in a theatrical production when the director and actors decide where to place an emphasis.

But even they are not in total control. S. L. Bethell, in *Shakespeare and the Popular Dramatic Tradition*, referred to the multi-conscious apprehension of the audience. The spectators of the play do not merely receive what is being presented to them by the action they are witnessing. They are also conscious of what is going on around them: the people next to them – talking, coughing, concentrating or restless – and whether they are watching in the open air or in a closed dark space, and (if in the former, as at the recreated Globe Theatre) whether a plane flies overhead or they feel drops of rain. However, it goes deeper than this, since the spectators bring to their own receptivity differences in attitude, gender, ideologies, education, class, problems and perplexities, desires and wishes. This results in a complex interaction occurring in what can be taken from the experience of watching the play itself. It is something present in any production of any play, but some plays have as a subject issues that can spread out across the audience, triggering divergent viewpoints such as those Drakakis delineates for *The Taming of the Shrew*. Further, a particular subject matter may be more divisive for an audience depending on the decade or even the year of a production.

As we will see in Chapter 7, interpretation and problems of sensibility are crucial to any modern reading of *The Merchant of Venice* because of its complex depiction of the Jew as an outsider in a dubious Christian society. *The Taming of the Shrew* may not be concerned solely with Kate, just as *The Merchant of Venice* is not concerned solely with Shylock. The probable diversity of audience responses to these plays sets difficult challenges for modern directors. Some directors of *The Taming of the Shrew*, such as Michael Bogdanov (RSC) or Jan Sargent (Newcastle upon Tyne) in the late 1970s, were encouraged by the play's fluidity and the productions' honesty to interpret it with a modern sensibility and perceive Kate as a victim. In doing so they may have closed off, however, the contextual social revelations going on elsewhere in the play, exposed, for example, by Baptista's rule over his family or by the relationships of Lucentio and Bianca or Hortensio and the Widow. Bill Alexander (RSC, 1992) was one director who effectively used the framing device of *A Shrew* in order simultaneously to conjure up a suspension of disbelief by creating layers of 'reality' – that of 'the theatre', of 'Sly', of "the hunting lords and ladies", of 'players as people', of actors 'acting'. At various points in the play, Sly, who remained on stage throughout, was drawn into the action of the main play, while at another time a question was directed to the audience in the theatre. The artificiality of the whole was exposed as the major element of comic interest, with the result that, perhaps, some of the more difficult questions raised by the play were obscured.

Jonathan Miller adopted a different strategy in an earlier RSC production (1987) by utilizing the conventions of Italian *commedia dell'arte* theatre, as though the roles in the play were all stock types appearing in a traditional popular theatrical form. Consequently, the foregrounding of theatrical convention neutralized the prospect of any ethical objection to the action of the story. In other words, Miller chose a different kind of framing story for the play but he could not avoid the duplication of the same issues that critics have identified as being central to the play. Playing the action in such a deliberately conventional mode may remind the audience that this is not something to be taken too seriously, but this strategy could be accused of making light of the serious social questions and of the ambiguity that modern critics and audiences have discovered in the play.

Another alternative means of interpreting the drama is to play it as the rumbustious work that it can be. This interpretation occurs in the famous film version starring Elizabeth Taylor and Richard Burton, which contemporary audiences were persuaded to think reflected the tempestuous nature of the two actors' own off-screen relationship. In this production there was probably some degree of blurring of reality and artificiality in the audience response, but even so the film's entertainment value has endured.

Interpretations of this drama, therefore, abound because a variety of levels of perception are being questioned. Is that brightness in the sky the moon or the sun? We name this phenomenon because we accept the referential relationship between the word 'moon' and the bright object that appears in the sky at night. But does the word point directly to the reality, and if so, how? In *Romeo and Juliet*, Juliet asks "What's in a name? That which we call a rose / By any other word would smell as sweet" (2.1.90–1). In *The Taming of the Shrew* Act 4 Scene 3 lines 28f, is the person on the road a beautiful young woman or an old man? How do you differentiate between the different elements of reality, and how do you represent reality? What is the relationship between words and actuality? Are words the instruments of will, and is dominant will determined in the end by those with most power, by a social stratification or by a tyrannical individual? And is that power something that can be imposed upon one human being by another, violently, or does power work through persuasion and agreement between the members of a society? In such a complex social organization, how can an individual survive or even overcome the obstacles placed in their way?

If the play asks such questions, do we have to look beyond the plot of the play itself to what it signifies, almost in the manner of a humanist parable? Petruchio, in naming the sun the moon or the moon the sun, declares:

Now, by my mother's son, and that's myself,
It shall be moon, or star, or what I list,
Or ere I journey to your father's house.

In her own interests, and for her own preservation, Kate is forced to acquiesce:

Forward, I pray, since we have come so far,
And be it moon, or sun, or what you please,
An if you please to call it a rush-candle,
Henceforth I vow it shall be so for me. (4.3.6–8, 12–15)

▲ A 2012 production of *The Taming of the Shrew*, with Samantha Spiro as Kate, behaving 'shrewishly', and Simon Paisley Day as Petruchio.

Living within a political tyranny, people rebel, or if they conform, they do so hypocritically or display a pragmatic ingenuity: Petruchio swears by the only thing of which he is sure, "by my mother's son, and that's myself". Shakespeare lived in such times. At the opening of this play, Petruchio and Kate are both rebels in their different attitudes to the prevailing social order. Kate behaving in an uncooperative manner ('shrewishly'), and Petruchio willing to violate social decorum. By the end they appear to have harmonized with one another to such an extent that they triumph in winning the bet and exposing the hollowness of the other characters' relationships. In fact, at the end of the play it is Bianca and the Widow who display, from within the institution of marriage, the very characteristics of shrewishness of which the dominant order disapproves.

Shakespeare leads us to this conclusion by allowing the main plot to develop through clear structural formula. The main narrative opens with a problem, this time not one associated with death but with the waywardness of a daughter rebelling against the legitimate will of her father. Kate's transformation from 'shrew' to obedient wife takes place within Petruchio's home in Verona and on the return journey to Padua. But it is in the unfolding structure of the play, and the series of comparisons and contrasts between the characters involved in their different courtship rituals, that a solution to the initial problem has gradually emerged. Kate may have been freed from her father's control but marriage imposes a new control upon her that seems to be either the same or harsher than the original restraint.

Here there is something intimidating in what Stephen Greenblatt terms "sexual energy". The sexuality of the bizarre relationship between Petruchio and Kate, appears violent. Yet gradually Kate accepts it as being infinitely better for her than the life that she had in the society which she has left and to which she now returns. Women in her father's value system are put up for auction and whoever bids the highest wins them. It is this society against which Kate rebels. The narrative never explains a particular cause, though she talks of revenge and also of favouritism. Bianca, as her name implies, is all white. Kate reproaches her father, although it takes the form of what we might call 'sibling rivalry' in which she is envious of Bianca's position in relation to her father's affections:

Nay, now I see
She is your treasure, she must have a husband,
I must dance barefoot on her wedding day,
And for your love to her lead apes in hell.
Talk not to me. I will go sit and weep
Till I can find occasion of revenge. (2.1.31–6)

Baptista ironically helps her to that "revenge" by his appeal to an external force. Petruchio is a benefactor who appears to have the power and the capacity to 'tame' Kate, although his first action after the marriage is to remove her from her father's house. This relieves Baptista of his problem daughter, but when Kate returns she is sufficiently reformed to be able to effect a triumph from within the structure of the patriarchal family. She is now one of the 'married women' and from that supposed dignity, as defined by the society that Baptista represents, she can exploit the situation at the dinner table. Petruchio wins the bet but so does she. The force (her husband), with whom she is now united, provides the opportunity for her to exact revenge on the representatives of the society against which she had initially rebelled. The question remains, however, has she been subdued or has she discovered a subversive strategy that will allow her to live in a society that subjects her to masculine control?

To dress Kate in sackcloth for her final speech is acceptable for a modern audience, but it may actually diminish the persuasive power of the parable that the structure and narrative enforces. Whereas the romantic comedies *As You Like It* and *Twelfth Night* conclude with celebratory affirmations of marriage, this play reveals the shallowness of a society that utilizes the rituals of romance but in a superficial manner. It channels Kate's rebellion into a victory for both her and Petruchio over, and yet seemingly within, existing social conventions. If Kate is willing to accept that the sun can be called the moon, then what 'truth' is there in her statement claiming "Thy husband is thy lord, thy life, thy keeper." (5.1.158)? It is only through mutual self-belief and an acceptance of their gendered social roles that Petruchio and Kate can triumph:

Come, Kate, we'll to bed.
We three are married, but you two are sped.
'Twas I won the wager, though you hit the white.
And being a winner, God give you goodnight! (5.1.196–9)

The innuendo is that Petruchio and Kate, having won, will have a better, i.e. a more 'truthful', marriage night than the other couples. Some modern sensibilities may not appreciate it but Kate is revenged and her rebellion has been successful. Pragmatically, and cleverly, she and her husband do more than just survive the deadweight of social convention, except that we cannot be finally certain that, as a modern audience, we can approve of this strategy or that everyone in the audience will be taking the same view. The comedy makes light of what for an Elizabethan audience was beginning to pose serious problems, and just as modern Feminism has demanded that we question the veracity of traditional gender relationships, and seek to reform them, so the play raises issues that matter to us certainly as much as they did to its original audiences.

The Merchant of Venice (1596–8)

In such a night
Did Jessica steal from the
wealthy Jew
And with an unthrift love did run
from Venice
As far as Belmont.

(5.1.18–21)

The Merchant of Venice (1596–8) is a complex and controversial play. Since the Jewish Holocaust, the play has provoked much debate about how it can be read or performed without causing unease. This is because it contains what some regard as overt anti-Semitism. The question that many critics ask is, whether in this play Shakespeare is confronting or pandering to the anti-Semitic prejudices of his audience or readers, historical or contemporary. I have discussed some of these issues in *Shakespeare and the Modern Dramatist* in relation particularly to two 20th-century dramatists, Charles Marowitz and Arnold Wesker, who deconstructed the Shakespearean text and reconstructed it afresh within the context of modern sensitivities. Similarly, Bill Overton in *The Merchant of Venice: Text and Performance* delineates "two main reasons why Shylock is a problem", the first being the historical context, and the second that the play must be "implicated in that history if it fosters anti-Semitism"[36]. In the discussion here, however, the play will be considered from two structural perspectives:

▶ it will locate the issues relating to Shylock the Jew within the context of Shakespeare's secularizing of a Roman Catholic sacramental convention, thereby critically polarizing two different cultures

▶ it will note how Shakespeare uses his comic formula in three interweaving plots which result in differing resolutions that may or may not satisfy audience expectations.

Much has been written on the historical context of Jewry in London at the time of the writing of the play, in particular the execution in 1594 of Dr Roderigo Lopez, Elizabeth I's physician, who was accused of trying to murder her. Julia Briggs points out that although critics have tended to assume that there were very few Jews living in London during the 1590s, they have not taken into account that Jews, like Roman Catholics, could not profess their faith openly. Indeed, she writes that many of them were European "converts" and had come from Spain:

> There may have been as many as 200 Jewish converts in England, working as doctors and in other professional or advisory capacities. Socially and physically they were virtually invisible, and this, along with their (usually) Spanish origins further contributed to the anxiety their presence aroused[37].

To be a Jew from Catholic Spain, the bitter enemy of Protestant England, was probably not something many desired to publicize. But it raised the possibility of dramatic conflict that was ripe for theatre. Thematically the Jew in Shakespeare's play dislikes the Christians as much as the Christians demonstrate that they dislike the Jews. Shylock refers to Antonio:

How like a fawning publican he looks!
I hate him for he is a Christian,
But more, for that in low simplicity
He lends out money gratis and brings down
The rate of usance here with us in Venice. (1.3.28–32)

Antonio is accused by him of spitting on "my Jewish gaberdine" and calling him "misbeliever, cut-throat dog", to which the Christian churlishly replies:

I am as like to call thee so again,
To spit on thee again, to spurn thee too.
If thou wilt lend this money, lend it not
As to thy friends ...
But lend it rather to thine enemy, (1.3.120ff)

And this is exactly what Shylock does, encouraging his 'enemy' Antonio in an agreement which, if taken seriously, will endanger the merchant's life. In the famous trial scene (Act 4 Scene 1), the Jew's demand for justice is counterbalanced by the Christian appeal for mercy. Antonio states:

You may as well do anything most hard
As seek to soften that – than which what harder? –
His Jewish heart: (4.1.79–81)

and Portia makes her great plea for Christian mercy which begins:

The quality of mercy is not strained,
It droppeth as the gentle rain from heaven
Upon the place beneath. (4.1.184f)

Shylock replies to all of this with "My deeds upon my head! I crave the law," (4.1.206), a statement that is a faint echo of the curse that, according to St Matthew's Gospel, the Jews called down upon themselves and their children in demanding Christ's blood: "His blood be on us and on our children!" (Matthew 27.25). When, however, Shylock finds himself frustrated by the law, the Christians taunt him and the limits of their mercy are exposed. The Jew is forced to bequeath his money to his daughter, who has rejected him and eloped with a Christian. Further, he is forced to convert to Christianity, just as some Spanish Jews may have done, although firm evidence of this is scarce.

There is no doubt that Shakespeare makes Shylock adamant in both his hatred and his desire for "his bond". But he is also depicted as a father deeply hurt by his daughter Jessica's elopement and her theft of some of his money and valued possessions, including his dead wife's ring (3.1.79–81). In Act 3 Scene 1, Shylock refers to his daughter in his description of what has happened as "My own flesh and blood to rebel!" and is taunted by the Christian Salerio, to whom he replies, "I say, my daughter is my flesh and blood" (3.1.24, 26). Here, Shakespeare is providing the actor with the opportunity to characterize Shylock's humanity as well as to expose the element of "flesh" and "blood" which will be his undoing. The Jew continues with the great speech in which he defends his decision to take revenge, by making Antonio "look to his bond" (3.1.33–4). He affirms his humanity:

> ... I am a Jew. Hath not a Jew eyes? Hath not a Jew hands, organs, dimensions, senses, affections, passions? ... If you prick us, do we not bleed? If you tickle us, do we not laugh? If you poison us, do we not die? And if you wrong us, shall we not revenge? (3.1.40ff)

This famous passage, however, raises a number of issues. Jonathan Bate reminds us that the reference to 'pricking' disassociates the Jew from witchcraft, since the pricking of the thumb without bloodshed was an Elizabethan proof of witchcraft. The opening line, though, would remind a Christian audience of the difference between the Old Testament 'an eye for an eye' operation of justice and the Christian teaching of love and mercy. The very thought of 'bleeding' presages the traditional predicament of the Jew in that his bond will demand the bleeding of Antonio, who is placed in a position similar to Christ before the Crucifixion. If you prick or pierce human flesh, then the blood will flow. So what will happen when you cut a pound of flesh from near a man's heart?

In his Introduction to the new Arden edition of the play, John Drakakis explains the foregrounded image of blood that occurs throughout the play:

> Blood is the bodily location of unrestrained carnal desire (the properties of youth but also the attributes of cultural otherness), and it also figures as the juridical absence that ultimately invalidates the Jew's bond[38].

Shylock's 'blood' makes him a 'stranger' within the Venetian community, the carnal blood of youth is restrained by Portia's dead father, but it also prompts Shylock's daughter's elopement with the Christian Lorenzo, which betrays her Jewish blood. This in turn, as Drakakis argues, allows the word 'flesh' to open "a series of conflicting meanings that reveal a struggle between a socially approved method of generation and a hellish aberration that biologically and fiscally perverts an accepted natural order"[39]. Salerio comments to Shylock:

There is more difference between thy flesh and hers than between jet and ivory, more between your bloods than there is between red wine and Rhenish. (3.1.27–8)

Such flesh and blood images expose many of the preconceptions of the play and prefigure the trial scene in which Christian and Jew face each other as representatives of opposing cultures. Flesh and blood imagery and Christian tradition and argument coalesce as the Antonio/Shylock narrative develops through the play.

In Roman Catholic teaching, at the moment of consecration in the communion service, or Mass, the bread and wine are believed to be transformed into Christ's body and blood through a mystical process for which the theological term is 'transubstantiation'. This sacrament is an outward sign of inward grace, received by the priests and dispensed to members of a congregation as holy communion. In the medieval church, however, the congregation would not always receive the sacrament and when they did, they would only receive the bread.

The Protestant Reformation questioned the whole notion of transubstantiation by refusing to accept that bread and wine were actually converted into the body and blood of Christ, but Venice, the setting of this play, was Catholic. In Shakespeare's England there would have been a residual memory of the Catholic teaching of transubstantiation. The argument for not receiving both the consecrated bread (body) and wine (blood) of Christ was simple: you could not receive the body without implicitly taking the blood since the two could not be separated. In a 15th-century play known as the *Croxton Play of the Sacrament*, some Jews steal the consecrated bread but as they try to desecrate it by stabbing at it, the bread begins to bleed. In the sacrament, the blood and flesh are so intertwined that to cut the latter is to let the former flow. Portia, Shakespeare's Italianate (Catholic) Christian from Belmont, may, in her defence of Antonio, be drawing on Catholic doctrine as well as medical fact to triumph over the Jew.

This Christian religious context, however, can be seen to go further in secularizing another theological point. In *The Stripping of the Altars*, Eamon Duffy reminds us that the sacrament of holy communion was "an image of forgiveness and grace, not of judgement". He points out that the Catholic faithful only took communion at Easter time, when it was called " 'taking one's right', a revealing phrase, indicating to take communion was to claim one's place in the adult community."[40]

This is illuminating in relation to *The Merchant of Venice*. Shylock's insistence on his taking of his "bond" or "taking his own right" in law may have fed off past cultural/religious contexts in its negative manifestation. In this instance it is not a communicant who is "taking his own right" through receiving the body and blood of forgiveness, grace and community, but a person hostile to Christian Venice – and therefore Catholic society – who wishes to take the flesh and therefore the blood of a member of the community to "bait fish withal" and "feed my revenge" (3.1.37). The fish is one of the earliest symbols of Christianity and of Christ himself. Shylock is not only the outsider in a Christian/Catholic community, foregrounding "judgement" over "forgiveness and grace" by a crude parody of the Mass, but a Jew deliberately trying to destroy the merchant Antonio because he is a Christian. Antonio, as the play emphasizes from the opening scene (1.1.137–41, 155–62) to the last scene (5.1.263–7), is prepared to sacrifice all he has, even his life, for the love of his friend. In Christianity, no man has greater love than he who lays down his life for his friend in imitation of Christ, who laid down his life for his love of all humanity. Shylock is frustrated in his "baiting of the fish" by the courtroom's secularized expression of Christian theology as well as the physical reality that if you cut the flesh, the body will bleed.

Shakespeare's conclusion of this critically controversial scene goes further in not fully condoning the Christian triumph. If, as Duffy holds, holy communion is not an image of judgement but of forgiveness and grace, at the end of this scene the Christians are exposed in the cruelty of their judgement and triumph since they demand of Shylock his very identity. He is forced to lose not only his possessions but the creed by which he lives and his identity as a Jew. Earlier in the play Tubal 'tortures' Shylock over Jessica's bad Jewish conduct (3.2). In Act 4 Scene 1, however, we have Shakespeare exposing the Venetians as bad Christians and also, Drakakis notes, as bad Venetians, since Venice was thought of as a place hospitable to 'strangers'.

In his Introduction to the New Penguin edition of the play, W. Moelwyn Merchant writes of Shylock's exit from the stage at the end of the trial scene as "one of the most puzzling moments on the Shakespearian stage"[41]. In defeat Shylock says tamely "I am content" (4.1.401) and asks leave to go, saying that he is "not well", just as Antonio and Portia in the early scenes of the play have been "weary". But then Shakespeare is silent, giving actors of the role an opportunity to improvise the character's departure from the stage. In Jonathan Miller's production (National Theatre, Old Vic, 1971–3) Laurence Olivier famously had himself, as Shylock, led off silently into the wings, after which the audience heard a howl of agony from backstage. What had these Christians done in their application of "mercy", which appears devoid of the necessary Christian attributes of forgiveness and grace?

In the production history of *The Merchant of Venice* there are examples, in the 19th century in particular, of the play ending at this point and of Act 5 being cut from the production. The play became almost the defeat, even the tragedy, of Shylock, as great actors such as Sir Henry Irving dominated the stage in the role. But an over-emphasis on Shylock risks making a travesty of this complex play, which has not one but a variety of interweaving plots.

The Merchant of Venice is necessarily a play with multiple endings as the various plots work themselves through in the context of the Shakespearean formula. The title of the play should not go unnoticed, since it foregrounds the merchant Antonio. Consequently a dominant aspect of the work is to do with the mercantile currency of trade: commodities and money. Bassanio's description of Portia is that "In Belmont is a lady richly left", although he adds "And she is fair and, fairer than that word, / Of wondrous virtues" (1.1.163–5). In Belmont, suitors have to choose between gold, silver and lead, with the Prince

▲ Sir Henry Irving as Shylock, a portrayal of which Bernard Shaw said: "There was no question then of a bad Shylock or a good Shylock: he was simply not Shylock at all ... he played in flat contradiction of the lines, and positively acted Shakespeare off the stage." Nevertheless, Irving played the part over a thousand times, to great acclaim.

of Morocco, another 'outsider' welcomed by an Italianate Christian society, learning the hard lesson that "All that glisters is not gold" (2.7.66).

This exposes another Renaissance issue. The doctrine of the sacrament as an outward and visible sign of inward, spiritual grace may have led to a convention within Elizabethan and Jacobean drama that an unattractive or 'different' apearance, perhaps because of physical disability or to the physical differences of race, may be a manifestation of monstrosity or evil. Another convention acknowledged that outward saintly show could mask inner evil. Shakespeare's own 'crookback', Richard III, and the pockmarked De Flores in Middleton and Rowley's *The Changeling* are prime examples of the former, whereas machiavellian figures like Duke Altofront in Marston's *The Malcontent* or Ulysses in Shakespeare's *Troilus and Cressida* are indicative of the latter.

Shakespeare in this regard appears to oscillate. In *Othello*, Shakespeare shows how the Venetians both use and abuse the black man, with the consequence that the dramatist generates sympathy for the outsider that may be akin to the manner in which Shylock exits from the stage. But earlier in *The Merchant of Venice*, as the Prince of Morocco is frustrated in choosing the gold casket and departs, Portia remarks "Let all of his complexion choose me so" (2.7.80). Is this a pandering to Elizabethan prejudices? With the dismissal of the next suitor, the Spanish Prince of Arragon, Bill Overton comments:

> *No modern audience can respond as an Elizabethan audience would have responded to a representative of the country which had recently tried to invade its own. It is difficult here to avoid the impression that Shakespeare gratifies contemporary prejudice*[42].

At the heart of the casket scenes is the question of the appearance of wealth as opposed to the dignity of the human being. Portia has been placed at the centre of a dangerous wager that will determine her future. Those who take on the wager and fail will suffer, but what would have happened to Portia if they had triumphed? The implication is in comedy that this will not happen, but through the various plots Shakespeare allows some undercurrents to rise to the surface. There is a certain cruelty involved in the accepted imposition of a dead father's will. John Drakakis notes that this exposes an interesting contrast with the Shylock/Jessica relationship:

> The living Jew's patriarchal authority is questioned in his own house, whereas the wisdom of the dead Christian father's word (and his meaning) is adhered to in Belmont[43].

In both locations, money is a motivating force. In the plot relating to Jessica and Lorenzo, for example, Jessica steals money and possessions from Shylock's house. In the merchant's plot, Antonio risks all his money in entrepreneurial ventures at sea and uses his own flesh as equity against the loan from Shylock. Money, therefore, dominates through to the last act, when Antonio fortuitously finds that his "ships / Are safely come to road" (5.1.302–3). Thus we have three interweaving plots in which money and equity are significant. In addition, there is a strange little subplot concerning the clown, Lancelet.

Each of the three plots uses the traditional Shakespearean comic formula. The first relates to Antonio and Bassanio. Antonio begins the play by stating a problem:

> *In sooth I know not why I am so sad.*
> *It wearies me, you say it wearies you;*
> *But how I caught it, found it, or came by it,*
> *What stuff 'tis made of, whereof it is born,*
> *I am to learn:*
> *And such a want-wit sadness makes of me*
> *That I have much ado to know myself.* (1.1.1–7)

Whilst his companions speculate that it's because he has risked all his fortune at sea, the audience may soon suspect that the truth of the sadness is tied up with his love for Bassanio. This is not necessarily because of Bassanio's "prodigal" (1.1.131) behaviour, which has wasted Antonio's previous loans to him, but because he has sworn "a secret pilgrimage" (1.1.122) to Belmont to woo Portia. Antonio is going to lose the man he loves and for whom he will endanger his life because of that love. He will pay for a journey and an adventure which may end in Bassanio's marriage. The geographical relocation of Bassanio to Belmont cannot solve the real problem for Antonio. It may result in a financial solution for Bassanio, allowing him to gain enough money to pay off his debts, but in doing so Bassanio will marry the wealthy woman and his friendship will be lost to the merchant. Shakespeare here is effectively distorting his formula to a point whereby there can be no resolution for Antonio, except in that his financial fortune is restored in Act 5. In the meantime, Bassanio chooses the right casket and wins Portia. But in the end Antonio, in having endangered his life for his love of Bassanio, is left a lonely figure on the stage, surrounded by the heterosexual reconciled and married couples.

Homosexuality is not explicit in the play but there are significant hints that it was written possibly around the same time as the narrative of Shakespeare's Sonnets. The love of two men for each other in the Sonnets and then the subsequent arrival of the dark lady may not be too far away from the narrative of *The Merchant of Venice*, although there is no suggestion in the play that Antonio has an affection for Portia. He remains steadfast in his love for Bassanio, for whom again he affirms he would lay down his life (5.1.263–7).

The second plot stems from the first; in Belmont, Portia's first appearance is made to correspond with the sadness of Antonio through her opening line: "By my troth, Nerissa, my little body is aweary of this great world" (1.2.1). Anxiety and weariness appear to be features of both Venice and Belmont, producing a correspondence between Antonio (the victim) and Portia (his eventual saviour). Bassanio's arrival and success in the caskets trial resolves that weariness for Portia in the way that it cannot for Antonio. Shakespeare then sets a further problem to be solved, which he has prepared in the opening scene. The news comes that Antonio's life is in danger. The result is the relocation of Portia and Nerissa, disguised as men, to Venice, where they not only resolve the problem of Shylock's bond and save Antonio's life, but also test the marital fidelity of their lovers, Bassanio and Gratiano. In tricking their husbands to give up the rings that their wives gave them at their betrothals, the women expose the fickleness and the masculine anxieties of both Bassanio and Gratiano, and they elicit a firmer romantic commitment from their spouses. The ring is a sexual symbol of the sanctity and fruitfulness of partnership. Once promised to the partner, the body is not to be given to another. The men have no right to give away the rings, the sexual symbolism of which is tied both to their marriage oaths and to the chastity of their wives. The rings are their outward signs of inward fidelity. Christian marriage is sacramental. Thus when Portia "discovers" that Bassanio has given his ring to the learned doctor she scolds:

Let not that doctor e'er come near my house.
Since he hath got the jewel that I loved, ...
I'll not deny him anything I have,
No, not my body nor my husband's bed. (5.1.235–6, 239–40)

The "jewel" is more than the ring. It is a vaginal symbol of her very self. It is all tame, bawdy comedy, of course, and the audience, having knowledge of the facts, are waiting for the comic recognition scene that soon follows:

You are all amazed.
Here is a letter, read it at your leisure.
It comes from Padua, from Bellario.
There you shall find that Portia was the doctor,
Nerissa there her clerk. (5.1.280–4)

All is resolved, except, as noted, for the continued loneliness of the merchant, Antonio.

The third interweaving story is the elopement of Jessica from Shylock's house, which she describes as "hell" (2.3.2). She disguises herself as a young man, escapes with Lorenzo and relocates to Belmont. In Act 5 Scene 1, these lovers cite examples of lovers in history, all of whom, however, were victims of tragedy: Troilus and Cressida, Thisbe and Pyramus, Dido and Aeneas, and Medea, who, though she helped her lover Jason's father Aeson, betrayed her own father in her elopement exactly as Jessica has done to her father. The opening of Act 5 is a beautifully poetic scene but with an undercurrent of some poignancy, noting through these references the fragility of love and relationships as a consequence of betrayal.

The comic subplot involves the clown Lancelet (whose name conjures up the adulterous lover Sir Lancelot of Arthurian legend) leaving his master Shylock's service for that of Bassanio. In Act 2 Scene 2, the clown plays a trick on his father Gobbo, leading him to believe his son "is indeed deceased, or as you would say in plain terms, gone to heaven" (2.2.40–1). It is a trick of deception that in other plays, from *Romeo and Juliet* to *The Winter's Tale*, is used by Shakespeare in a much more significant way but here it is used as a comic interlude, testing and commenting on the emotional aspect of relationships. Love is about sharing a common truth, not about deception. In *Measure for Measure* (1604) such a deception, a major element of the plot, is to form the kernel of a darker exposé of relationships and their manipulation.

The Merchant of Venice uses three interweaving plots and comic episodes to make its dramatic progress. It delves into issues of race and religion, of conduct and belief, of trust and oaths, mercy and justice, love, identity, lack of grace and faithfulness, of sacrifice, pain and compensation. It is not a play to be reduced to black and white judgements. Maybe it is a play which tries to do too much, leaving certain issues to perplex the actor, audience or reader. But however complex and however controversial it proves to be, *The Merchant of Venice* is one of Shakespeare's greatest plays, moving and manipulating his comic formula to great dramatic effect. In this respect it is a fitting play with which to start to draw to a close this short study of Shakespeare's comedies in the All That Matters series, since the six plays we have considered appear to deal very much with things that mattered in Shakespeare's day and continue to matter in our own time.

Conclusion:
Language and song

*Mark how one string, sweet
husband to another,
Strikes each in each by mutual
ordering,
Resembling sire and child and
happy mother
Who, all in one, one pleasing
note do sing,*

Sonnet 8, lines 9–12

In this short study an attempt has been made to open up the issues of Shakespeare's plays through looking at the ways in which they work, examining the formula that provides a foundation for them, and the interaction of plot and structure that opens out to varieties of possible themes. Shakespeare is not a didactic poet and dramatist; rather he is one who commentates through narrative, refusing time and again to make judgements, although, like all of us, he may sometimes fall into the trap of doing so. He is conditioned by his own historical reality, living at a particular time, but his plays are not set in stone.

Plays can be interpreted in performance in different ways, allowing a variety of meanings to emerge from the texts themselves and their performances. They can change in texture, colour and sensitivity depending on the cultural demands of successive ages and the cultures that present and receive them. It is this malleability within the works that can frustrate those who are looking for definitive answers. There are few, if any, such answers since in his mimetic examination of the human predicament, he asks questions and poses problems without forcing opinions. This gives the opportunity for others to impose their views, as the original performance scripts can, to an extent, bend subtly without breaking.

This malleability applies also to one aspect that so far has not been discussed but which underlies the entire discourse. The plays are written predominantly in verse. Shakespeare is a poet, and in the 21st century, an age relatively unaccustomed to verse-speaking or reading poetry, it is his verse which can frighten potential audiences.

At the end of the 20th century, before the revolution in social networking using modern communication technologies, one might have argued that the contemporary age was predominantly a visual rather than a verbal one. But new technologies have restored the force of the written word and the need to be concise in, for example, the word limitation imposed by Twitter. Ironically, Shakespeare's verse form stems from a similar need for discipline. He uses a rhythm of language that imitates speech, employs discipline and yet still allows a malleability within that discipline.

The basic poetic line is the iambic pentameter. What that term signifies is a ten-beat line in which the words are stressed in a soft/hard, soft/hard, soft/hard, soft/hard, soft/hard pattern. Just saying the words "soft, hard" in this way gives the line rhythm. This rhythm can be changed, as it might be in music, to produce a particular effect. The famous opening line of *Richard III*, "Now is the winter of our discontent", starts hard/soft and then continues on the regular pattern. In the same speech Shakespeare elongates line 16, where Richard refers to his own deformity, "I, that am rudely stamped, and want love's majesty", in order to mimic that deformity by deforming the line.

In his sonnet sequence Shakespeare disciplined what he wanted to say in a poem into just 14 lines. The sonnet came from Italy and its form became known as the Petrarchan, after the Italian poet Petrarch. It was constructed as an Octave and a Sextet. The eight-line Octave has two four-line stanzas, with a repeating rhyme structure in alternate lines. To understand this, we assign a letter to the rhyming word at the end of each line. So the Petrarchan Octave rhymes abab abab. This is followed by the Sextet, which has its own rhyme scheme; this may be cde cde, or cdc cdc, or cde dce. Generally, the Octave presents a problem or an issue which the Sextet reinforces, eases or solves.

Some Elizabethan poets, most significantly Shakespeare, varied this structure to develop three four-line distinctive quatrains followed by a two-line couplet. For example, these would be rhymed as first quatrain abab; second quatrain cdcd; third quatrain efef with a concluding couplet as gg. The quatrains present the narrative or issue and the couplet sums it up or pithly comments upon it. This form is usually known as the Shakespearean sonnet.

Shakespeare was certainly writing or had written some of his sonnets at the time that he wrote most of the plays discussed in this book. The disciplined structure of the Shakespearean sonnet, and possibly the knowledge of the Petrarchan sonnet, has an affinity at least with the need for the structured discipline discussed in the composition of the comedies. Whether the sonnets are autobiographical or whether they are a fictional creation by a poet who was also a dramatist has been and continues to be a matter for debate.

Successful art is disciplined. It is not haphazard. Sometimes it may appear simple to the point where people will say "Well, I could paint like that." But of course they cannot, since beneath the apparent simplicity (or indeed masked complexity) is the experience of trial and error and the knowledge of the artistic laws that pertain as well as the skill of the artist. Great artists often show the courage to push such laws to their limits or to develop new ones. Writing can be a journey through which the artist has to travel, sometimes with pain and anguish, as he or she strives for a finished product. We may detect fictional or real personal pain in the Shakespearean sonnets as we do in some of the comedies, as earlier chapters have shown. The pain is that of the passing of time, of the transience of youth, of mutability and of loss. That, however, is matched in some of the comedies and the sonnets by a celebration of the progress of relationship building and the sustainability of the art itself. This is stated, for example, in Sonnet 55, the last eight lines of which are:

Nor Mars his sword, nor war's quick fire shall burn
The living record of your memory.
Gainst death and all oblivious enmity
Shall you pace forth, your praise shall still find room
Even in the eyes of all posterity
That wear this world out to the ending doom.
So, till the judgement that yourself arise,
You live in this, and dwell in lovers' eyes.

It is the poem, the art, the play that transcends the ravages of time and which provides an immortality until the world itself disappears. This Shakespearean sonnet begins by stating its theme:

Not marble nor the gilded monuments
Of princes shall outlive this powerful rhyme.

The communicative vehicle of the plays is language. Through words the plays have to create images in our minds as well as carry the narrative forward, or build up character or the communication between characters. Shakespeare tells us that the language has to work on our "imaginary forces" (*Henry V*, Prologue, line 18), setting place and tone. Thus in *A Midsummer Night's Dream*:

> *I know a bank where the wild thyme blows,*
> *Where oxlips and the nodding violet grows,*
> *Quite over-canopied with luscious woodbine,*
> *With sweet musk-roses and with eglantine:*
> *There sleeps Titania sometime of the night,*
> *Lulled in these flowers with dances and delight:*
> *And there the snake throws her enamelled skin,*
> *Weed wide enough to wrap a fairy in.* (2.1.254–61)

Even modern visual technology might find it difficult to present such an imaginary picture as Shakespeare has Oberon deliver here. With the plays in performance, however, the poetry is not the only vehicle of communication. As well as conjuring up the imagery of the language, Shakespeare is producing a script for the actors: speaking, moving, sitting, standing, and interacting with each other, with the physical elements on the stage itself, the theatre and the audience of which you are a member. Shakespeare realizes the force of the complex communicative vehicle and his art is to use it, bringing the various elements together. In this he has a mastery. Note, for example, in the tragedy *Hamlet*, how Hamlet, when talking in prose to Rosencrantz and

Guildenstern, uses the physical stage – thrusting out into the auditorium as a "promontory" with the painted "canopy" above leading to the sky that can be seen over the open-air part of the theatre – to communicate a further revelatory intensity in character and yet simultaneously, possibly, undercut that intensity through humorous insults:

> ... I have of late – but wherefore I know not – lost all my mirth, forgone all custom of exercise; and indeed it goes so heavily with my disposition that this goodly frame, the earth, seems to me a sterile promontory, this most excellent canopy, the air, look you, this brave o'erhanging firmament, this majestical roof fretted with golden fire, why, it appears no other thing to me than a foul and pestilent congregation of vapours. (2.2.278–84)

▲ The reconstructed Globe Theatre in London, showing the thrust stage and canopy, and the openness to the elements.

Here he is probably linking the sky to the paintings on the canopy of the thrust stage, which is surrounded by the "congregation" of the audience, breathing their 'pestilence' of air, which in time of plague would close the theatres. The communicative vehicle is moving around the physical environment of the stage and theatre and involving the audience, who might well react to the actor as he refers directly to them, identifying them as "foul and pestilent". Such an interaction of actor and audience, with implied comic banter, may cause a dramatic effect which would be contrary to a romantic, empathetic or mere sentimental reading of the lines.

In comedy, likewise, Shakespeare is not averse to self-referential humour, laughing at his own mastery of poetic language as, for example, in *Love's Labour's Lost*, Act 4 Scene 3, when the male lovers read out their sonnets, not to the women they love but directly to the audience, to great comic effect in performance.

It is often held that in these plays the characters who are of inferior social status speak in prose, and to some extent that is the case, as with the Mechanicals in *A Midsummer Night's Dream*. Bottom in his 'audition' for the Pyramus and Thisbe play aspires to speak verse, and the result allows Shakespeare to mimic the bombastic lines of some of his contemporary dramatists:

The raging rocks
And shivering shocks
Shall break the locks
Of prison gates.
And Phibbus' car

Shall shine from far
And make and mar
The foolish Fates. (1.2.21–8)

Humorously, Shakespeare has Bottom sum up his recitation with the words "This was lofty" and then the character returns to his normal prose (1.2.29f). Roger Warren, in *A Midsummer Night's Dream: Text and Performance*, draws on David P. Young's view that "although the usage is by no means strict, we associate blank verse with Theseus, Hippolyta, and the courtly world ...; couplets with the lovers ...; lyrical measure ... with the fairy world; and prose with the mechanicals."[44]. Warren notes that "Shakespeare handles these various styles with equal fluency ... ease and clarity."[45]

This distinction within language function, however, is not always the same throughout the plays. Sometimes, for example, prose is used to increase the emotional impact of what is being said by a central character, as with Shylock's affirmation of his humanity and of his sense of injustice at the way, it is implied, his nation has been persecuted by the Christian culture:

He (Antonio) hath disgraced me, and hindered me half a million, laughed at my losses, mocked at my gains, scorned my nation, thwarted my bargains, cooled my friends, heated mine enemies, and what's the reason? I am a Jew. (*The Merchant of Venice*, 3.1.37–40)

In *As You Like It* Rosalind speaks much of her part in prose, perhaps bringing a more immediate attempted realism to what is happening behind her contrived and controlling, romantic narrative. It is such variations that allow modularities in tone, creating atmosphere, leaving ambiguities hanging in the air for the audience to savour in the richness of the dramatic progress or experience, as, for example, in Viola's concealed admission of her love for Orsino in *Twelfth Night*:

Viola: *... She never told her love,*
But let concealment, like a worm i'th 'bud,
Feed on her damask cheek: she pined in thought,
And with a green and yellow melancholy
She sat like patience on a monument,
Smiling at grief. Was not this love indeed?
Orsino: *But died thy sister of her love, my boy?*
Viola: *I am all the daughters of my father's house,*
And all the brothers too, and yet I know not. (2.4.113–18, 122–4)

This rich passage, brim-full of image and gentle ambiguity, permits a softness of empathetic humour for the audience, whose knowledge of what is going on is greater than that of either character. The language referring to melancholy itself brings out the warm melancholy of the play's action. Similarly the dramatist introduces mime and song to great effect in *Twelfth Night*, reinforcing the play's action and thereby inviting participation in that action, as when Feste sings of the transience of youth:

O mistress mine, where are you roaming?
O stay and hear, your true love's coming, ...
What is love? 'Tis not hereafter
Present mirth hath present laughter.
What's to come is still unsure,

In delay there lies no plenty,
Then come kiss me, sweet and twenty,
Youth's a stuff will not endure. (2.3.26–7, 34–9)

This has not always been the perception through the centuries. Lois Potter comments: "Though everyone who sees the play notices how important songs are for its atmosphere, it would have been hard to discover this before the twentieth century."[46] She notes that the songs 'O mistress mine' and 'Come away, come away, death' were not sung in the 18th century and the final song, 'When that I was and a little tiny boy', "reappeared only in 1763".

In the Shakespeare script, however, music appears to be played in order to complement the poetry and the prose. In *Much Ado About Nothing*, Act 2 Scene 3 line 48, Benedick humorously questions: "Is it not strange that sheep's guts should hale souls out of men's bodies?" but later he is forced to ridicule himself in his own attempt at wooing through song or poetry, reflecting "No, I was not born under a rhyming planet, for I cannot woo in festival terms" (5.2.26–7). It may be that Richard Burbage, the actor who played the part of Benedick originally, had no singing voice and was also being gently laughed at by the playwright. When Will Kempe left the company in 1598, Robert Armin, a singer, took over the role of clown with the effect that more music appears to have been written into the plays.

One of the best ways to get to grips with Shakespearean verse, its technicality and malleability is to read passages aloud. Shakespeare's contemporary John Marston wrote that his plays were written to be performed, not read, and so it was in the case of Shakespeare, who, as far as we know, did not see any of his plays into print in the way that both Marston and Ben Jonson did. As we have seen, scholarship has tended over the years unconsciously to underplay the performance aspect in its attempts to evaluate these plays' literary merits. The result has been almost to imprison Shakespeare in an elitist culture. But Shakespeare's profession was far from being elitist. He needed a popular audience in order to earn his living. There are some lines which now are almost impenetrable without footnotes and scholarship. *Love's Labour's Lost* is particularly difficult in this respect but it can still be understood if, as readers or a theatre audience, we do not get bogged down in the minutiae of scholarship. The progress, the fluidity, the movement of the whole is greater than the particularity of certain words, phrases or lines. We have to let the play run in our reading in order to allow it to work.

In everyday speech we allow the flow of conversation. Few of us can actually recount every word exactly as spoken once the conversation has come to a close, but we are aware of the tenor and nature of what has occurred. We start to understand great art in the same way but then we recall moments of real significance that stand out through the clarity and beauty of their expression.

In an increasingly materialistic and violent world, where spiritual values have been eroded, art, music, literature, dance and theatre remind us of the qualities as well as the infirmities of the human condition. They cause us to pause, and as a consequence they matter in affirming the very positive nature of the artistic endeavour. In the sonnets Shakespeare affirms his belief in the longevity of that endeavour. No doubt many ages may have conceived of themselves as increasingly materialistic and violent but have also found affirmation in creativity both for themselves and as a guarantee of the future. This is why governments and societies neglect art at their peril. Shakespeare's language, Shakespeare's poems and plays are part of the fabric of history, not a history that is restricted to a particular century or a particular world, but a history of performance and reading that has helped form ideas and fine-tune perceptions through the centuries. Sometimes these ideas have been inappropriate and, as we have seen, we have to ask questions about the propriety for us of plays as radical as *The Merchant of Venice*, but on the whole in their affirmation of their art and in their self-reflective responsibility the plays make us think, so at least we smile when Fabian comments:

If this were played upon a stage now, I could condemn it as an improbable fiction. (*Twelfth Night*, 3.4.97–8)

This self-referential understanding and the humour in the comedies are concerned with life, and that is why Shakespeare can and does matter, if we want him to do so.

Ten key biographical dates

1 **1564** Shakespeare is born, 23 April(?). Christened at Holy Trinity Church, Stratford-upon-Avon, 26 April.

2 **1582** Shakespeare marries Anne Hathaway.

3 **1583** Daughter Susanna is born.

4 **1585** Twins Hamnet and Judith are born.

5 **1595** Shakespeare named as one of the players performing before Elizabeth I; Shakespeare is by now an established actor and writer.

6 **1596** Son Hamnet dies; buried in Stratford-upon-Avon, 11 August.

7 **1597** Buys New Place (two cottages and two barns) in Stratford-upon-Avon.

8 **1600/1** *Hamlet* is performed. John Shakespeare, William's father, dies (1601).

9 **1608** Granddaughter Elizabeth Hall is born; christened 21 February. Shakespeare's mother, Mary (Arden), dies; buried 9 September.

10 **1616** Daughter Judith marries Thomas Quiney, 10 February. William Shakespeare dies, 23 April(?), aged 52; burial recorded at Holy Trinity Church, 25 April.

Ten key historical dates of Elizabeth I's reign

11 **1564** Michelangelo dies; Galileo born; Shakespeare born; Christopher Marlowe born.

12 **1576** James Burbage opens The Theatre, the first professional theatre in England.

13 **1577** Francis Drake circumnavigates the world, returning in 1580, when he is knighted by Elizabeth I.

14 **1587** Mary, Queen of Scots is executed.

15 **1588** Defeat of the Spanish Armada.

16 **1592** Plague in London; playhouses are closed for two years.

17 **1593** Playwright Christopher Marlowe killed in Deptford, 30 May.

18 **1598** Rebellion in Ireland.

19 **1601** Earl of Essex's rebellion and execution.

20 **1603** Death of Elizabeth I (acceded 1558); accession of James I, son of Mary, Queen of Scots.

Ten key historical dates of James I's reign (1602–25)

21 **1605** Gunpowder Plot, an attempt by Catholic gentry to blow up James I and Parliament, fails.

22 **1607** Virginia, the first English colony in North America, is established.

23 **1611** Publication of the Authorized Version of the Bible.

24 **1613** The Globe theatre burns down.

25 **1616** Shakespeare dies. Ben Jonson publishes his own works in Folio.

26 **1618** Execution of Sir Walter Raleigh. Thirty Years War begins in Europe.

27 **1620** The *Mayflower* sails to New England, where the Pilgrim Fathers establish a colony.

28 **1621** The poet John Donne becomes Dean of St Paul's Cathedral.

29 **1623** First Folio of Shakespeare's Complete Works is published by Heminges and Condell.

30 **1625** James I dies; accession of Charles I (executed 1649).

Ten London playhouses of the Shakespearean period

31 **The Theatre** (1576–98), Shoreditch. The first public professional playhouse in London, built by James Burbage north of the City.

32 **Blackfriars** (1576–94, 1596–1655), near Ludgate Hill. Smaller interior theatre, its satirical plays often got it into trouble. Shakespeare's company took it over in the early 17th century.

33 **The Curtain** (1577?–1622?), Bishopgate. Built in north London, not far from The Theatre.

34 **The Rose** (1587?–1605/6), Bankside. Built by 'entrepreneur' Philip Henslowe.

35 **The Swan** (1595–1621?), Bankside. Johannes de Witt famously sketched this theatre around 1596, commenting that it held 3,000 persons, but his sketch and account are not totally reliable.

36 **The Globe** (1599–1613, 1614–44), Bankside. Built by Shakespeare's company on the south bank of the Thames, east of The Swan. Peter Streete was the master carpenter. It burnt down during a performance of *Henry VIII* on 29 June 1613. The new theatre was opened in 1614. In 1997 a replica was opened on London's South Bank as near as possible to the original site.

37 **The Fortune** (1600–21, 1623–62?), Finsbury. Built by Henslowe and Alleyn to rival The Globe, using the same carpenter, Peter Streete; the contract between them still exists. The original building burnt down in 1621.

38 **Red Bull** (1605?–63?), St John Street, Clerkenwell.

39 **Hope** (1613/14–17), South Bank. Reportedly used as a bear garden in 1617.

40 **Phoenix (Cockpit)** (1617–65?), Drury Lane. A private indoor theatre. Private theatres were more expensive than public theatres but didn't necessarily discriminate according to class; anyone who could afford admission could attend.

Ten(+) modern theatres for Shakespearean performance

41 **The Royal Shakespeare Theatre(s)**, Stratford-upon-Avon. Home of the Royal Shakespeare Company.

42 **The National Theatre(s)**, South Bank, London. Rivals the RSC in the intellectual and artistic quality of its productions.

43 **The Globe Theatre**, London. Established to develop productions in an environment as close to their original as possible. Stand or sit, but the back and feet can ache however good the performance!

44 **The Old Vic**, London. A historic theatre that kept Shakespeare 'alive' during the Second World War, it was the home of the National Theatre until the South Bank complex was built.

45 **Folger Shakespeare Theatre**, Washington DC, attached to the Folger Shakespeare Library. Long the home of Shakespearean productions in the US capital, it presents four plays a year, usually all by Shakespeare. The company and director vary from show to show.

46 **Stratford Ontario Festival Theatre**, Canada. World-renowned festival venue, engaging distinguished actors.

47 **The Young Vic**, London. Shakespeare productions here can be outstanding.

48 **The Royal Exchange**, Manchester, and **The Liverpool Everyman** are both good provincial theatres, unafraid to produce interpretations rivalling the two big companies, as is also the case with the **Donmar Warehouse** in London.

49 **Birmingham Repertory Theatre** has been a nursery theatre for Stratford in years gone by. It recently reopened after refurbishment and is adjacent to the City of Birmingham Library, which houses an important Shakespearean library.

50 **Clwyd Theatre Cymru**, Mold, Wales. Fortunate to have had some excellent directors, including currently Terry Hands, former artistic director of the RSC. If Shakespeare is in the season, it is worth a visit.

Ten(+) renowned Shakespearean actors

(**Note:** This list is of actors since the time of Richard Burbage (1558–1619), but includes only actors who are no longer alive. A companion volume in this series, *Shakespeare's Tragedies*, lists renowned contemporary actors.)

51 **Thomas Betterton** (1635–1710). Son of a cook to Charles I, acted for Davenant's company. Played roles such as Toby Belch, Mercutio, Falstaff, Othello and Hamlet.

52 **David Garrick** (1717–79). One of the most famous actors of all time, who organized the Shakespeare Jubilee in 1769. He was the manager of Drury Lane Theatre, a playwright, editor of Shakespeare and actor, who developed a more natural style of acting than hitherto seen. His roles included Hamlet, Richard III, Hotspur, King Lear, Romeo, Macbeth, Benedick and Antonio.

53 **Charles Macklin** (1700–97). Transformed the portrayal of Shylock in *The Merchant of Venice* by foregrounding the villainy of the character. He discarded the red wig traditionally used as a sign of the Jew, replacing it with a red hat. He was particularly renowned as Iago in *Othello*.

54 **Edmund Kean** (1787–1833). A romantic actor, sometimes seen as self-indulgent, but excelled in roles such as Macbeth, Othello, Richard III and Shylock. His son **Charles Kean** (1811–68) was a compelling actor, playing, for example, Richard II, Richard III, Shylock, King Lear and, notably, Leontes in *The Winter's Tale*.

55 **William Macready** (1793–1873). Playing Shylock, he attempted to find a greater psychological consistency in the character than Edmund Kean, believing in the character as a person with whom he had to gain affinity. As such he was starting to prefigure acting styles to come at the turn of the century. He reinstated *King Lear* as a tragedy in 1838, rescuing it from the Nahum Tate version of 1681 (which had ended the play happily, with Lear resuming the throne) and returning it to something like the original. Also played Benedick, Coriolanus, Hamlet, Henry V, Macbeth, Othello and other roles.

56 **Henry Irving** (1838–1905). Probably the most famous 19th-century actor, and the first actor to be knighted. As

Shylock, he introduced a new scene into *The Merchant of Venice* in which he silently entered the stage after Jessica's elopement. He was popular in the role, playing it over a thousand times. Other famous roles included Hamlet, Lear and a 'neurotic interpretation' of Macbeth.

57 **Frank Benson** (1858–1939). He consolidated and ran the Stratford-upon-Avon Festival, which eventually led to the establishment of the Shakespeare Memorial Theatre/Royal Shakespeare Theatre and the Royal Shakespeare Company. For much of his career he played at Stratford, appearing in the great roles.

58 **John Gielgud** (1904–2000) and **Laurence Olivier** (1907–89). The two dominant figures of the 20th-century stage. Gielgud was known for his Benedick, Romeo, Hamlet, Lear and Leontes; his Stratford Othello was not a success. Olivier was the founder of the National Theatre and formerly artistic director of the Chichester Festival. He was somewhat mannered, as can be seen in his film portrayal of Othello, but highly regarded for his stage Hamlet, Othello and in particular his Coriolanus at Stratford. During the Second World War he used Shakespeare as part of the war effort, particularly with his film of *Henry V*. His film version of *Richard III* is possibly the most quoted film performance in history.

59 **Michael Redgrave** (1908–85). One of the 20th century's greatest Hamlets, a radical portrayal but one which, ironically, came to be seen as 'traditional', as the RSC developed. Redgrave had himself advocated a faithfulness to the dramatist in acting. Other roles included Benedick, Hotspur and Shylock.

60 **Paul Scofield** (1922–2008). After making his name at the old Birmingham Repertory Theatre, he progressed to Stratford and beyond. His King Lear for Peter Brook, (Stratford, 1962) was one of the most famous of the 20th century, and he played Hamlet in Stratford and Moscow. He had a distinctive voice and delivery.

Ten renowned Shakespearean actresses

(Note: This list is of actresses since the boy actors of the Shakespearean period, but includes only actresses who are no longer alive. A companion volume in this series, *Shakespeare's Tragedies*, lists renowned contemporary actresses.)

61 Elizabeth Barry (1658–1713). Reputedly a fine tragic and melodramatic actress of the Restoration period. She appeared with Betterton. She had an affair with the poet Lord Rochester, giving birth to a daughter.

62 Sarah Siddons (1755–1831). Renowned for her Lady Macbeth and Queen Katharine in *Henry VIII*. She also excelled as Desdemona and Ophelia. Sir Joshua Reynolds famously painted her as the Tragic Muse.

63 Dorothea Jordan (1761–1816). A sensational, scandalous actress who was the mistress of the Duke of Clarence, later King William IV. Acted at Drury Lane, playing major female roles in Shakespearean comedy: Olivia, Rosalind, Beatrice and Imogen. Riots sometimes broke out during her performances.

64 Ellen Tree (1805–80). The wife of Charles Kean, she played Lady Macbeth, Desdemona and Hermione.

65 Ellen Terry (1847–97). One of the greatest actresses. She worked with Irving and notably played Portia to his Shylock. She was also known for her Beatrice in *Much Ado About Nothing*. She is one of the giants of the English stage but was also famed in America, where she often appeared.

66 Sarah Bernhardt (1844–1923). Hugely talented French actress, who famously played the role of Hamlet in an adaptation and as Cordelia in a French-language production.

67 **Sybil Thorndike** (1882–1976). Significant in keeping Shakespearean productions alive during the Second World War by playing male roles. She played most of the principal Shakespearean female roles and was renowned for her Lady Macbeth.

68 **Edith Evans** (1888–1976). Well-known for her Lady Bracknell in the film of Wilde's *The Importance of Being Earnest* and particularly for the delivery of the line 'A handbag?'. She was a towering theatrical figure known for her portrayal of Rosalind, Portia and Beatrice and also for the Nurse in *Romeo and Juliet*.

69 **Vivien Leigh** (1913–67). Famous for her role in *Gone with the Wind*, she played Lady Macbeth to her husband Laurence Olivier's Macbeth and Ophelia to his Hamlet. She was also known for her Viola, Juliet and Cleopatra.

70 **Peggy Ashcroft** (1907–91). A much loved actress of stage, cinema and television, with a quiet dignity and presence. She was one of the troupe that with Sir Peter Hall developed the RSC, becoming an associate director. She excelled particularly as Queen Margaret in the RSC's acclaimed 'The Wars of the Roses' cycle of history plays. Throughout her career she played the major Shakespearean parts: Portia, Viola, Cordelia, and was Juliet in the production in which Olivier and Gielgud alternated the roles of Romeo and Mercutio. She was acclaimed as Beatrice to Gielgud's Benedick.

Ten(+) film/TV/DVD productions

71 **The Comedy of Errors** (1978). A television production by Trevor Nunn based on his famous musical RSC production of the play. Directed for television by Philip Casson, the cast includes Judi Dench, Michael Williams, Roger Rees and Mike Gwilym.

72 **Much Ado About Nothing** (1993). A film directed by Kenneth Branagh, with Kenneth Branagh, Richard Briers, Emma Thompson, Denzel Washington, Keanu Reeves, Michael Keaton, Ben Elton and Kate Beckinsale. Despite some embarrassingly forced humour in the Dogberry–Verges scenes, this is a lively screen rendition, its famous opening shots immediately engaging and exciting.

73 **A Midsummer Night's Dream** (1996). This is the film/TV version of Adrian Noble's excellent RSC production of the play, adapted and directed by Noble. The cast includes Paul Arnott, Alex Jennings, Lindsay Duncan, Barry Lynch and Desmond Barrit. The film is as magical as the original theatre production. Also unmissable is the Michael Hoffman film (1999) with Michelle Pfeiffer, Christian Bale, Rupert Everett, Calista Flockhart and Kevin Kline.

74 **As You Like It** (2006). The production, adapted and directed by Kenneth Branagh, has a Japanese setting which really doesn't work, but the play survives the imposition. Try the Globe Theatre performance of 2010.

75 **Twelfth Night** (1996). An intelligent screen version directed by Trevor Nunn, based on his RSC production, with Imogen Stubbs, Helena Bonham Carter, Toby Stephens, Mel Smith, Richard E. Grant, Nigel Hawthorne, Imelda Staunton and Ben Kingsley.

76 **Twelfth Night** (1988). Another good production by Kenneth Branagh, who deserves accolades for bringing so much Shakespearean drama to the modern cinema and media. The cast includes Richard Briers, Anton Lesser, Frances Barber, Caroline Langrishe and Christopher Ravenscroft.

77 **The Merchant of Venice** (1973). An ITV transmission adapted and directed by John Sichel, based on the National Theatre production directed by Jonathan Miller, with Laurence Olivier and Joan Plowright. This contains

Olivier's famous departure from the trial scene and off-stage 'howl'.

78 **The Merchant of Venice** (2004). A screen version directed by Michael Radford with an excellent cast including Al Pacino, Lynn Collins, Jeremy Irons and Joseph Fiennes.

79 **The Taming of the Shrew** (1967). The famous Zeffirelli film with Richard Burton and Elizabeth Taylor. Among many screen adaptations of the play are the musical *Kiss Me Kate* and *10 Things I Hate About You* (1999), directed by Gil Junger, with Heath Ledger and Julia Stiles.

80 **Playing Shakespeare** (1982). Master classes by RSC veteran director John Barton with a host of great RSC actors, including Judi Dench, Ian McKellen, Patrick Stewart, Ben Kingsley, Alan Howard, David Suchet, Richard Pasco, Susan Fleetwood, Jane Lapotaire, Sínéad Cussack, Sheila Hancock, Lisa Harrow, Barbara Leigh Hunt, Michael Pennington, Donald Sinden, Michael Williams, Mike Gwilym and Norman Rodway. A compelling insight into the directors' and actors' art.

20 Questions

(For answers, see end of Suggested further reading section.)

81 'Two Gentlemen of _ _ _ _ _ _' ? – fill in the blank with the name of the city.

82 Name two of Olivia's suitors in *Twelfth Night*.

83 When Petruchio and Kate argue in *The Taming of the Shrew* (4.3) about the sun and the moon, they are on a journey from which city and to which city?

84 In which play does Fabian appear?

85 What is the name of the Roman dramatist, two of whose plays were a source for *The Comedy of Errors*?

86 In which year did Shakespeare's son die and what was his name?

87 Name the two principal 'clown' actors in Shakespeare's company.

88 Identify the fourth age of man.

89 What is the name of Sir Rowland de Bois' second son?

90 'A _ _ _ _ _ _ come to judgement!' Fill in the missing name.

91 Name one of the Shakespeare comedies in this book that features a shipwreck.

92 Who were John Heminges and Henry Condell?

93 Portia is the name of a character in *The Merchant of Venice*, but in which other Shakespearean play does a character of the same name appear who 'fell distract' and 'swallowed fire'?

94 In which play does Egeon appear, and in which Egeus?

95 In *A Midsummer Night's Dream* Hippolyta marries … ?; Helena marries … ?; Hermia marries … ?

96 Who played Shylock in Jonathan Miller's famous National Theatre 1971–3 production of *The Merchant of Venice*?

97 According to Orlando, although time moves on, what is absent from the Forest of Arden?

98 The play 'What You Will' is usually known as … ?

99 Which British theatre director, who founded the Royal Shakespeare Company, stated that Shakespeare's comedies are about 'growing up'?

100 Fill in the blank: "In this same interlude it doth befall / That I, one _ _ _ _ by name, present a wall."

Notes

Chapter 1

1 Ben Jonson's poem 'To draw no envy ...', lines 116, 142, in the Preliminary Matter to the First Folio; see Jonathan Bate and Eric Rasmussen (eds), *The RSC Shakespeare: The Complete Works* (Basingstoke: Macmillan, paperback edition, 2008), pp. 61–2.

2 Michel Foucault, *The Archaeology of Knowledge* (trans. A. M. Sheridan Smith; London: Tavistock, 1972), p. 103.

3 Deborah Cartmell and Michael Scott (eds), *Talking Shakespeare: Shakespeare into the Millenium* (Basingstoke: Palgrave, 2001), pp. 13–14.

Chapter 2

4 Stanley Wells, *Shakespeare for All Time* (London: Macmillan, 2002), p. 132.

5 R. A. Foakes, *Arden Shakespeare: The Comedy of Errors* (London: Methuen, 1962), Introduction.

6 Stephen Greenblatt, *Will in the World* (London: Jonathan Cape, 2004), pp. 130–1.

Chapter 3

7 In John Drakakis (ed.) *Alternative Shakespeares* (London: Methuen, 1985), p. 145.

8 *The RSC Shakespeare: The Complete Works*, pp. 365–6.

9 M. C. Bradbrook, *English Dramatic Form* (London: Chatto & Windus, 2nd impression, 1970), p. 14.

10 C. L. Barber, *Shakespeare's Festive Comedy* (Princeton, NJ: Princeton University Press, 1959), p. 124.

11 Ibid, p. 139.

12 *Alternative Shakespeares*, p. 188.

13 Ibid, p. 177.

14 Harry Levin, *Signet Classics: The Comedy of Errors* (London and New York: New American Library, 2nd revised edition, 2002), Introduction.

15 William Empson, *Some Versions of Pastoral* (London: Chatto & Windus, 1935), p. 34.

16 Barber, p. 158.

17 *Alternative Shakespeares*, p. 75.

Chapter 4

18 Michael Scott, 'Shakespearean Choice and Current Practice', *Critical Survey*, vol. 5, no. 3, 1993, pp. 313–22.

19 Ibid, p. 320.

20 Malcolm Evans, *Signifying Nothing: Truth's True Contents in Shakespeare's Text* (Brighton: Harvester Press, 1986), pp. 145–6.

Chapter 5

21 *Complete Works*, Introduction, *Twelfth Night*, p. 646.

22 Peter Davison, *Hamlet: Text and Performance* (1983), p. 38.

23 Barber, p. 241.

24 Barber, p. 245.

25 Stephen Greenblatt, *Shakespearean Negotiations. The Circulation of Social Energy in Renaissance England* (Oxford: Clarendon Press, 1992), p. 72.

26 Kiernan Ryan, *Shakespeare* (Basingstoke: Palgrave, 3rd edition, 2002), p. 25.

27 Peter Hall, *Making an Exhibition of Myself* (London: Sinclair-Stevenson, 1993), p. 134.

28 Ibid, p. 135.

29 Stanley Wells, *Royal Shakespeare* (Manchester: Manchester University Press, 1977)

30 James Shapiro, *1599: A Year in the Life of William Shakespeare* (London: Faber, 2005), p. 370.

Notes

Chapter 6

31 Quarto 1594, *The Taming of A Shrew*, The Malone Society Reprints, vol. 160, 1998, pp. 51–2.

32 H. J. Oliver, Introduction, *The Oxford Shakespeare: The Taming of the Shrew* (Oxford: Oxford University Press, 1982) p. 43.

33 Juliet Dusinberre, *Shakespeare and the Nature of Women*, (London: Macmillan, 1975), p. 108.

34 Marilyn French, *Shakespeare's Division of Experience* (London: Cape, 1982) p. 317.

35 Ibid, p. 329.

Chapter 7

36 Bill Overton, *The Merchant of Venice: Text and Performance* (Basingstoke: Macmillan, 1987), p. 24f.

37 Julia Briggs, *This Stage-Play World: Texts and Contexts, 1580–1625* (Oxford: Oxford University Press, 1997), p. 100.

38 John Drakakis, *Arden Shakespeare: The Merchant of Venice* (London: Bloomsbury, 2010), p. 35.

39 Ibid, p. 76.

40 Eamon Duffy, *The Stripping of the Altars: Tradition and Religion in England c.1400–c.1580* (New Haven and London: Yale University Press, 2nd edition, 2005), p. 94.

41 W. Moelwyn Merchant, *New Penguin Shakespeare: The Merchant of Venice* (London: Penguin, 2005) p. 32.

42 Overton, pp. 20–1.

43 Drakakis, p. 77.

Chapter 8

44 David P. Young, *Something of Great Constancy: The Art of A Midsummer Night's Dream* (New Haven and London: Yale University Press, 1966), p. 66.

45 Roger Warren, *A Midsummer Night's Dream: Text and Performance* (Basingstoke: Macmillan, 1983), p. 12.

46 Lois Potter, *Twelfth Night: Text and Performance* (Basingstoke: Macmillan, 1985), p. 36.

Suggested further reading

Barber, C. L., *Shakespeare's Festive Comedy* (Princeton, NJ: Princeton University Press, 1959)

Bate, J., *The Genius of Shakespeare* (London: Picador, 2008)

Bate, J., *Soul of the Age: The Life, Mind and World of William Shakespeare* (London: Penguin, 2009)

Bethell, S. L., *Shakespeare and the Popular Dramatic Tradition* (London: P. S. King and Staples, 1944)

Bradbrook, M. C., *English Dramatic Form* (London: Chatto & Windus, 2nd impression, 1970)

Briggs, J., *This Stage-Play World: Texts and Contexts, 1580–1625* (Oxford: Oxford University Press, 1997)

Bryson, B., *Shakespeare* (London: Harper Press, 2007)

Cartmell, D. and Scott. M. (eds), *Talking Shakespeare: Shakespeare into the Millenium* (Basingstoke: Palgrave, 2001)

Charlton, H. B., *Shakespearian Comedy* (London: Methuen, 2nd edition, 1938)

Dollimore, J. and Sinfield, A. (eds.), *Political Shakespeare: New essays in cultural materialism* (Manchester: Manchester University Press, 1985)

Drakakis, J. (ed.), *Alternative Shakespeares* (London: Methuen, 1985)

Dusinberre, J., *Shakespeare and the Nature of Women* (London: Macmillan, 1975)

Evans, M., *Signifying Nothing: Truth's True Contents in Shakespeare's Text* (Brighton: Harvester Press, 1986)

French, M., *Shakespeare's Division of Experience* (London: Cape, 1982)

Frye, H. Northrop, *A Natural Perspective: The Development of Shakespearean Comedy and Romance* (New York: Columbia University Press, 1965)

Greenblatt, S., *Shakespearean Negotiations: The Circulation of Social Energy in Renaissance England* (Oxford: Clarendon Press, 1992)

Greer, G., *Shakespeare's Wife* (London: Bloomsbury, 2007)

Hawkes, T., *Meaning By Shakespeare* (London and New York: Routledge, 1992)

Jardine, L., *Reading Shakespeare Historically* (London and New York: Routledge, 1996)

Jones, E., *Scenic Form in Shakespeare* (Oxford: Clarendon Press, 1971)

Kott, J. (trans. B. Taborski), *Shakespeare Our Contemporary* (London: Methuen, revised edition, 1967)

Lerner, L. (ed.), *Shakespeare's Comedies: An Anthology of Modern Criticism* (London: Penguin, 1967)

Ryan, K., *Shakespeare* (Basingstoke: Palgrave, 3rd edition, 2002)

Scott, M., *Renaissance Drama and a Modern Audience* (London: Macmillan, 1982)

Scott, M., *Shakespeare and the Modern Dramatist* (Basingstoke: Macmillan, 1989)

Shapiro, J., *1599: A Year in the Life of William Shakespeare* (London: Faber, 2005)

Shapiro, J., *Contested Will: Who Wrote Shakespeare?* (London: Faber, 2010)

Vickers, B., *Appropriating Shakespeare: Contemporary Critical Quarrels* (New Haven and London: Yale University Press, 1993)

Wilson Knight, G., *The Wheel of Fire* (London: Methuen, 4th edition, 1954)

Answers to 20 Questions

81 Verona.

82 Duke Orsino, Sir Andrew Aguecheek, Malvolio.

83 From Verona to Padua.

84 *Twelfth Night*.

85 Plautus.

86 1596, Hamnet.

87 William Kempe (d. 1608) and Robert Armin (c.1568–1615).

88 Soldier (*As You Like It*, 2.7.152).

89 Jaques de Bois.

90 Daniel (*The Merchant of Venice*, 4.1.223).

91 *The Comedy of Errors*, *Twelfth Night*.

92 Fellow actors in the same company as Shakespeare, responsible for the publication of the first collection of his works, the First Folio, in 1623.

93 *Julius Caesar* (4.2.229, 230).

94 Egeon in *The Comedy of Errors*; Egeus in *A Midsummer Night's Dream*.

95 Hippolyta marries Theseus; Helena marries Demetrius; Hermia marries Lysander (*A Midsummer Night's Dream*, 4.1.172–4).

96 Sir Laurence Olivier.

97 A clock: "You should ask me what time o'day: there's no clock in the forest" (*As You Like It*, 3.2.230).

98 *Twelfth Night*.

99 Sir Peter Hall.

100 Snout (*A Midsummer Night's Dream*, 5.1.156–7).

Picture credits

The author and publisher would like to give their thanks for permission to use the following images:

The First Folio, Victoria and Albert Museum, London: Andreas Praefcke (in public domain)

The Comedy of Errors © Rex Features/Geraint Lewis

A Midsummer Night's Dream © Rex Features/Ronald Spencer/Associated Newspapers

As You Like It © Rex Features/Alastair Muir

Twelfth Night © Rex Features/Alastair Muir

The Taming of the Shrew © Rex Features/Alastair Muir

Henry Irving as Shylock (*The Merchant of Venice*) © Rex Features/Universal History Archive/Universal Images Group

The Globe Theatre, London © Rex Features

Acknowledgements

This book could not have been written without the help of my wife, Eirlys, to whom I am very grateful. My thanks go also to Professor John Drakakis, who kindly read through the typescript and made helpful suggestions which I have incorporated into the text. My thanks go also to my publisher Sam Richardson my editor Hilary Marsden and my agent Charlotte Howard for their encouragement. The book can serve as no more than an introduction. The reason why Shakespeare matters lies in the works themselves.

Index